THE OLD
Waldorf-Astoria
BAR BOOK

THE OLD
Waldorf-Astoria
BAR BOOK

• •

With AMENDMENTS due to
REPEAL of the XVIIIth

• •

Giving the Correct Recipes for FIVE HUNDRED COCKTAILS
and MIXED DRINKS known and served at the World's Most
Famous Brass Rail before Prohibition, together with More
than ONE HUNDRED ESTABLISHED FORMULAS for Cocktails
and Other Beverages, Originated while
Prohibition was in Effect

• •

*The Whole Flavored with Dashes of History
Mixed in a Shaker of Anecdote and Served with a
Chaser of Illuminative Information*

BY

ALBERT STEVENS CROCKETT
(HISTORIAN OF THE OLD WALDORF-ASTORIA)

Martino Publishing
Mansfield Centre, CT
2015

Martino Publishing
P.O. Box 373,
Mansfield Centre, CT 06250 USA

ISBN 978-1-61427-805-4

© *2015 Martino Publishing*

Cover design by T. Matarazzo

Printed in the United States of America On 100% Acid-Free Paper

THE OLD
Waldorf-Astoria
BAR BOOK

———•———

WITH AMENDMENTS DUE TO
REPEAL OF THE XVIIITH

———•———

Giving the Correct Recipes for FIVE HUNDRED COCKTAILS
and MIXED DRINKS known and served at the World's Most
Famous Brass Rail before Prohibition, together with More
than ONE HUNDRED ESTABLISHED FORMULAS for Cocktails
and Other Beverages, Originated while
Prohibition was in Effect

———•———

*The Whole Flavored with Dashes of History
Mixed in a Shaker of Anecdote and Served with a
Chaser of Illuminative Information*

BY

ALBERT STEVENS CROCKETT
(HISTORIAN OF THE OLD WALDORF-ASTORIA)

DODD, MEAD AND COMPANY
NEW YORK   1 9 3 4

PRINTED IN THE UNITED STATES OF AMERICA
BY THE VAIL-BALLOU PRESS, INC., BINGHAMTON, N. Y.

RECALLING

CERTAIN GENTLEMEN OF OTHER DAYS,

WHO MADE OF DRINKING

ONE OF THE PLEASURES OF LIFE—

NOT ONE OF ITS EVILS;

AND

WHO, WHATEVER THEY DRANK,

PROVED ABLE TO CARRY IT,

KEEP THEIR HEADS

AND REMAIN GENTLEMEN,

EVEN IN THEIR CUPS.

THEIR EXAMPLE

IS COMMENDED

TO THEIR

POSTERITY

CONTENTS

vii

I. PREAMBULARY

DURING what facetious American newspaper columnists sometimes referred to as the Period of the Great Drought—that is to say, during the days of the Noble Experiment—the art of mixing cocktails as known and practiced up to 1919 lapsed into a sort of desuetude, even if that could not be described as "innocuous" or even as innoxious.

In those larger times when legal liquor could be had more or less freely in this country, if one had the price, or was fortunate enough to be declared in by some host standing treat, new drinks owed their invention either to unusually enterprising barmen, or to customers gifted with imagination and longing for new savors and flavors or, possibly, the inspiration was attributable to what they had already drunk. Here and there one knew some amateur experimenter whose chief indoor sport was putting together new and sometimes weird and even terrifying concoctions and trying the result upon his friends. During the decade and a half preceding the Great War, "Have you tried this one?" was almost as frequent a prelude to something as "Have you heard this one?"

The war in Europe definitely diminished creative activities in the cocktail line. From London we heard that Britishers, drawn into the combat, had taken to drinking champagne, and were even being weaned away from their Scotch. When the A.E.F. discovered France, a simultaneous discovery was made of the wines of the country, together with what was quantitatively described as *"beau-coup cognac."* When the survivors of the War and its attendant gustatory campaigns got back home, it was to a country all set for strict Constitutional sobriety, legally enforced. America was to be dried up.

Of course, no such thing happened, except in theory. Sumptuary legislation has always proved repugnant to free men and difficult to enforce. Instead of becoming alcoholically arid, the United States grew wetter and wetter as the years passed. The bootlegger, once among the most despised members of society, became important—as important in his way as the Missing Link might be considered by ethnologists and anthropologists of the Darwinian school. Indeed, he proved a missing link. He bought magnificent motor cars or high speed motor boats, amassed fortunes, grew into might and acquired a definite and even respectable status as an indispensable member of society. More than one read his name in some Social Roster, —though it had probably been printed there before he turned outlaw. The racketeer and the gangster, protected by the politician and even in collusion with the revenue officer, waxed powerful and became superior to the law. The average American who wanted liquor bought from one or the other. What he got was their business, not his. True, persons with long purses might purchase what was "good stuff" according to pre-war standards, but mistakes were made. The rest of us often paid fancy prices for labels. Stimulated by the very difficulties created by the law and encouraged by the ease with which those difficulties could be surmounted, as well as by the temptation to break a statute that was never popular in large centers of population, an appetite for strong drink spread among the young, not sparing young women. It became "smart" to affect the speakeasy and to make it a place of assemblage; and "drunk" and "souse" became humorous rather than disreputable terms.

But avast with moral discussions! The story has been written, and we are trying to recover from what in effect was a national spree—with headaches, and sometimes worse. The fact was that, deprived of legal liquor, we had embarked, as it were, upon an unknown sea of alcoholic beverages. Thirsts were drowned, rather than quenched, in "bathtub" or synthetic gin—that or "whiskey" made from supposedly denatured wood-alcohol. Fatalities were frequent. The cocktail, long considered an aid to good appetite and digestion and cheer, often proved an enemy to digestion, health, morals and even mind. In sum, the art of drinking, according to the tenets of the long established American School, was lost, except one found in Havana, or Nassau, or elsewhere abroad, some veteran barman whose training and experience qualified him to compose drinks in the old, standard American way. The men employed in speakeasies to mix cocktails and other drinks as a rule knew nothing about the job and did not have valid liquors to start with. A "cocktail" was apt to prove just something with so-called gin in it, or a mixture of two or more of the imitations that masked behind well-known names.

Self-respecting bartenders of the old day—or most of them—had found other means of earning a living. Some had emigrated. There were exceptions. Breaking the law of the land—a frequent avocation for many of us—most of our social clubs found employment for experienced barmen. But rare it was that this particular searcher for truth and good spirit, who, through the courtesy of friends was enabled to sample the offerings of many club bars, tasted a cocktail that seemed authentic. And he never drank a cocktail at a club bar during the prohibition era without wondering whether it would prove his last.

Neighboring countries benefited much from prohibition in the United States. For Canada the Yankee tourist trade proved a great boon. From early spring to late autumn the roads carried northward hosts of automobilists, bent, not upon seeing the natural and other wonders of the Dominion so much as on sampling the spirituous fare available to any comer. Usually their first port of call, once across the border, or after registering at a hotel, was a government liquor store, which exhibited a generous desire to accommodate, despite the legal limitations on sales to a single customer. All one had to do was to go back as early and as often as he pleased. A late afternoon in a Montreal hotel usually yielded ebullient evidence of a heavy American invasion, which proclaimed to all within ear-shot that it had got what it had come for.

Certain steamship companies finally awoke to the possibilities that lay in catering particularly to our denied and increasing demand for good liquor and plenty of it; and week-end cruises, swift turn-about jaunts to the tropics and return "voyages to Nowhere" won enormous popularity and helped erase some of the "red ink" into which the trans-Atlantic steamship companies had sunk until they were almost awash. Many who embarked on such cruises later yielded curious descriptions of the foreign ports they had visited, telling of a Havana that was paved with sawdust and contained mostly within "Sloppy Joe's"; and a tour of the British West Indies often seemed to linger in memory mostly as a series of dashes from a table to the bar of "Dirty Dick's," in Nassau. It came to be said that a ship's company in those days did not disembark upon arriving back in New York, but was poured out upon the pier.

When the repeal of the prohibition amendment was accomplished, on December 5, 1933, proprietors of New York hotels and restaurants made the discovery that good bartenders, men who knew anything at all about mixing cocktails, were scarce. Most of the old-timers had died off, or forgotten what they had known. Steamships and clubs were raided; barmen were even imported; but it is a good hazard that out of every ten men employed to mix cocktails on that historic day of Repeal, not more than one really knew the rudiments of his trade. Schools for bartenders had sprung up, but they could not turn out experts fast enough to qualify. Properly mixing a wide variety of cocktails requires much more than a month of training. Long practice is absolutely essential.

Besides, even in pre-prohibition days, no one man could keep all the drink recipes in his head. Few latter-day cocktail slingers really have any conception of the number and variety of cocktails and other mixed drinks that used to be in demand. In order to be able to serve the correct cocktail when a customer called for his fancy of the moment, recipes had been written down and kept ready for consultation.

During the last few years, the market has been flooded with so-called cocktail recipe books. Without challenging them all, one may mention that some seem to have been based on the practices and even on the orthography of speakeasy "bar-keeps." In one, for example, I came across the recipe for a "Dacqueri"—presumably intended for "Dai-quiri," but whose formula would not be recognized as such anywhere in Cuba, where the rum it contains is the national drink. Not long ago, I made an examination of one volume which, judging from the quantity of names displayed, offered a tremendous number of cocktail recipes of startling variety. I found fewer than seventy whose names and formulas were known to me. Out of that seventy, the recipes for not as many as ten agreed with the formulas of pre-war times that were in my possession. They brought up Pickwickian memories.

"It depends, my lord," said *Mr. Weller*, during the trial of Bardell *vs*. Pickwick, "upon the taste and fancy of the speller."

Back in softer-boiled days and for more than twenty years, New York boasted many well run and well known bars, and one in particular that was famous all over the world. Everybody from everywhere who wanted the best of drinks, made according to the best traditions of the American School, found his way to it when he reached New York and carried away memories of it. In far-off Shanghai, in Peking, in Singapore, in Melbourne, in Cape-town, in Johannesburg, in Aden, in Calcutta, an American traveler was sure to find in a local club or hotel somebody who would boast of having had such-and-such a cocktail in the Old Waldorf-Astoria Bar. If the new acquaintance was a Scot, he was apt to lick reminiscent chops over the generous free lunch there dispensed.

The barmen in that historic dispensary—an even dozen of them when good times made good business—had to know what was what when it came to mixing and serving drinks. As at most first class bars of the period, all recipes were written down once they had been invented and tasted. Every new recipe brought to the bar must pass a try-out before it was inscribed in the Bar Book. It is to the fact that one of the Old Waldorf barmen held on to the copy of that Bar Book long after prohibition had shut what had grown by repute to the dignity of an American institution that we owe the preservation of the names and the real recipes of the authentic cocktails and most of the recognized mixed alcoholic drinks of ante-prohibition days. That barman was Joseph Taylor, who had been "called to the Bar" during its early days and who helped close it. He remained in the employ of the Old Waldorf-Astoria until its last day, working in what became known as its "beverage department" and handling no more stimulating potations than aerated water, ginger ale and near-beer. After the old hotel was closed, in 1929, Taylor was out of a job for a time, finally obtaining precarious employment until the opening of the new Waldorf. His self-respect would not permit him to work in a speakeasy, he told me. He used to call upon me at intervals. The last time was about ten months before Repeal Day. He was then looking forward eagerly, he said, to the return of old times, and to getting back behind a counter and plying the cocktail shaker in the old way, with "real stuff" to pour into it from genuinely labeled bottles. But he did not live to see that day.

The Old Waldorf Bar Book he had given me to use as I saw fit when I was writing the history of the Old Waldorf Bar—which I had known from shortly after its opening until the end—and in it I incorporated the contents of the recipe book. That book was intended simply as a contribution to the social history of an age—one I had treated from other standpoints in another volume, PEACOCKS ON PARADE, earlier published. When OLD WALDORF BAR DAYS came out, few Americans dreamed that repeal was hardly more than two years off. And so, while I "translated" and more or less codified and put into alphabetical order the contents of that battered, dog-eared little album, its pages stained with many samples of liquors, and which would probably show under a microscope the thumb prints of many barmen who had had to consult it, I had no idea of turning out a guide of any sort. I merely incorporated it as something that might interest the researcher into American *mores*, who, I felt sure, would find much material therein, and so permitted myself very little elaboration.

However, the book attracted wide and favorable comment. As Repeal Day approached, critics and connoisseurs who knew good liquors and particularly what cocktails used to be like, found that, by virtue of having been long in actual daily use, here was an authoritative compendium of the authentic cocktails of a by-gone day. True, its availability was handicapped by being tacked on, as it were, to a quasi-historical narrative and exposition, so that those who merely saw the book and the title did not readily guess, as a rule, that it contained a collection of cocktail recipes. Because of the book's history, it stood alone. It should be improved, amplified as much as necessary, and made thoroughly understandable and useful.

This was emphasized by Mr. Howard L. Lewis, Secretary of Dodd, Mead and Company. So that the author, encouraged and stimulated by the interest of a publishing firm of such high reputation and standing, gladly undertook the work of revision.

Besides the revised formulas for cocktails and other mixed drinks contained in the Old Waldorf Bar Book, I have included a number of recipes for other standard cocktails and mixed drinks, mostly gathered outside of the United States, and many of them tested and approved by the author.

II. CONSTITUTIVE AND DERIVATIVE

THE cocktail, as many generations have known it, is a distinctively American drink. Its name, its formulas and its influence as well, have been spread by traveling Americans to every corner of the globe. Or else Britons, bound for some distant part of an empire on which the sun is always setting, learned a recipe in an American bar and made the barman at the club in their remote destination experiment until he had achieved something like the flavors of the mixture whose tastes and effects they longed to experience again.

At home—in London, or wherever he dwelt in his tight little island—the Englishman as a rule did not succumb easily to the innovation. For many years the fact that the cocktail was an American drink was sufficient to condemn it in his eyes. The Britisher stuck to his Sherry or his Scotch or Brandy-and-Soda. So that the spread of the cocktail in anything like its pristine purity, so to speak, was due in greatest measure to peripatetic Yankees, some of whom never found any strange place liveable, or even bearable, unless or until they could get their cocktails when they wanted them.

Not until the present century was ending its second decade was it possible anywhere in the London the compiler of this volume knew—and that was considerable— to buy a genuine cocktail made in the American way. In Paris, yes. The French, making early discovery that profit lurked in catering to thirsts hostile to claret or Burgundy, imported cocktail shakers and increased the manufacture of ice. Not a few Frenchmen had learned about cocktails in America. The Chatham bar and Henry's and a dozen or more other places knew just how Martinis and Old-Fashioneds were made, and served them. That was one reason why many an American found Paris more enjoyable than London, and stayed longer. Of course, in London hotel bars frequented by Americans, cocktails, so-called, were served long ago by English barmaids and drunk liberally. American visitors, though they refused to acquire the tea habit and balked at Scotch, simply had to drink something in that climate. But somehow the concoctions lacked authenticity; they did not taste like real cocktails. English bartenders and barmaids, it appeared, found as much difficulty composing cocktails harmoniously as did their musicians in learning to play music of American origin and tempo. At this distance and with the conquest of London by our "jazz kings" a part of ancient history, the comparison must seem inept. But I knew the London of twenty-five to thirty years ago; I lived there.

Not until the summer of 1920, so far as I was able to ascertain, did an American-trained barman make his appearance at one of the high-class London hotels. That was the year when most American bartenders found themselves out of jobs. This one, however, was a Britisher. I knew the Englishman who had been commissioned by the management of that hotel to find such an expert in New York and happened to be in the lobby when the result of the mission was announced. I sampled one of the newcomer's first cocktails made on British soil.

Out in the Far East, the American Navy, true to tradition, did its share in spreading the gospel of the cocktail.

Certainly whatever may have been lacking in the results of their missionary endeavors up to the Spanish-American War was made up in 1898, just before and after Dewey's capture of the Spanish fleet in Manila Bay and during the Boxer Rebellion a few years later. Whatever the oft-encountered sign "American Bar" may have lacked in authentic backing when one encountered it in Europe, out in what were known as the Treaty Ports of China, in Yokohama and such other places in the Orient as our sailors, marines and soldiers came to know, one could find his Martini or any other cocktail that was in vogue back in the States.

Yet, while the cocktail is an American invention, its derivation and first date of application are hazed by anecdote and fancy. Take, for example, a story once heard in the Orient.

"A cocktail?" the Mandarin repeated, eying the drink doubtfully.

"Yes," replied the Standard Oil man, his host in Hong Kong.

"But why the name?"

The other shook his head. "Drink it and you will find the rooster feathers growing on you."

The Mandarin drank, perplexed. Having drunk, however, his curiosity over the name left him. All he wanted was another of the same. Soon afterward began in the Far East a demand for bottled Martinis and Manhattans, which did more to Americanize the Chinese than any other influence.

There was once a day when women did not drink cocktails. They even hesitated to pronounce the name. Over here we spoke of "roosters." Of course everybody knew that roosters had tails and it was a common opinion that the effect of a cocktail was to make the imbiber feel somehow like a rooster with his tail stuck up. Anyhow, if the cocktail was properly made, it had the effect of at least stimulating the appetite. But that much admitted, the derivation is still an open question and the date undecided.

As my habit, when at a loss for the origin of a word, is to appeal to one of the foremost lexicographers in our land, I put the ancestry of "cocktail" up to Dr. Frank H. Vizetelly, managing editor of the Standard Dictionary. Then it developed that even that eminent root specialist found himself stumped when it came to pinning an exact date on the word and getting down to the bottom of its family tree. But Dr. Vizetelly was kind enough to go into the matter with great thoroughness.

"The *cocktail*," Dr. Vizetelly replied, "goes back at least to the beginning of the 19th century, and may date back to the American Revolution. It is alleged by one writer to have been a concoction prepared by the widow of a Revolutionary soldier as far back as 1779. He offers no proof of the statement, but a publication, 'The Balance,' for May 13, 1806, describes the *cocktail* of that period as 'a stimulating liquor composed of spirits of any kind, sugar, water and bitters. It is vulgarly called "bitter sling," and is supposed to be an excellent electioneering potion.'

"Washington Irving, in 'Knickerbocker' (1809), Page 241, said of the cocktail: 'They (Dutch-Americans) lay claim to be the first inventors of the recondite beverages, cock-tail, stone-fence, and sherry cobbler.' Hawthorne referred to *cocktails* in 'The Blithedale Romance' (1852), as did Thackeray in his 'The Newcomes' (1855), but neither of these authors sheds any light upon the origin of the term.

"The New English Dictionary on Historical Principles says that the origin of the word *cocktail* is lost. In this connection, one writer refers to the older term *cocktail*, meaning a horse whose tail, being docked, sticks up like the tail of a cock. He adds: 'Since drinkers of cocktails believe them to be exhilarating, the recently popular song, "Horsey, keep your tail up," may perhaps hint at a possible connection between the two senses of "cocktail." '

"Bartlett in his 'Dictionary of Americanisms' gives the following: '*Cocktail*'—A stimulating beverage, made of brandy, gin or other liquor, mixed with bitters, sugar and very little water. A friend thinks that this term was suggested by the shape which froth, as of a glass of porter, assumes when it flows over the sides of a tumbler containing the liquid effervescing.' He quotes the following from the *New York Tribune* of May 8, 1862: 'A bowie-knife and a foaming cocktail.' In the Yorkshire dialect, *cocktail* described beer that is fresh and foaming.

"Brewer, in 'A Dictionary of Phrase and Fable,' following the definition of *cocktail*, adds the note: 'The origin of the term is unknown. The story given in the *New York World* (1891) to the effect that it is an Aztec word, and that 'the liquor' was discovered by an Aztec noble, who sent it by the hand of his daughter Xochitl to the King, who promptly named it "xoctl," whence "cocktail," is a good specimen of the manufacture of etymologies.'

"As you will see from the foregoing," Dr. Vizetelly concludes, "altho many theories have been advanced as to the etymology of the term *cocktail*, these, like most etymologies of the kind, are mere flights of fancy, and while they make interesting reading, can not be accepted as reliable."

So much for derivation and history. Now for the meaning of cocktail. The Standard Dictionary gives it as "[U. S.] A drink made of spirits mixed with bitters, sugar and flavor."

Well, that's sufficient to start with. But it was not a speakeasy definition during prohibition, and millions of Americans have grown up with very different ideas. In the Old Waldorf Bar Book, bitters of one kind or other was considered a necessary ingredient of most Gin cocktails. The favorite was Orange Bitters, which appears in something like one hundred different recipes. A distant second was Angostura. Then there were Calisaya, Boonekamp, Boker's, Amer Picon, Hostetter's, Pepsin, Peychaud, Fernet Branca, and so on. The Bitters was used in small quantities, ordinarily described as "one dash" or "two." But Bitters used to contain alcohol and prohibition made most brands illegal to import. One well known firm which specialized during prohibition in importing liquors whose alcoholic content had been reduced until they could be brought in as "flavoring extracts," told me it had not imported Orange Bitters in fourteen years.

The original Old Waldorf Bar Book contained almost three hundred cocktail recipes. That means more than appears, for of cocktails made with Vermouth there were frequently two variants, an ordinary and a "dry"—or "sec." That was particularly true where the recipe called for Italian Vermouth. Using French Vermouth instead, the result was a "dry" cocktail, one that was not sweet and a better appetizer. Certain barmen claimed to make a dry cocktail simply by increasing the proportion of Gin.

Many recipes, however, call only for French Vermouth. Gin was the base, or one of the bases, of approximately one hundred and fifty cocktails—more if the "dry" variants of cocktails are considered as different entities. In making forty or so, Whiskey was the base. Rum of one sort or another was used only in fourteen; for Bacardi and Jamaica—though the latter was the favorite indulgence of many of our colonial forefathers—had not attained the wide acquaintance among Americans the latter now enjoy. In this book, Cuban and Jamaican drinks of today are taken up exhaustively following the contents of the Old Waldorf Bar Book. Sloe Gin was the base of eleven recipes. There were forty-four whose base was either Brandy or one of a number of cordials. Frequently two or more were mixed. Other bases were Applejack or Apple Brandy, Calisaya, Dubonnet, Sherry, Port and Swedish Punch.

During the first two decades of the century, the commonly accepted American definition of a cocktail was a mixture of Gin and Vermouth with Bitters, iced and shaken. Of course, Whiskey cocktails had their many and ardent devotees; and the Manhattan, based on Whiskey, was a popular drink. To a big majority, however, Whiskey was something that should be taken neat, or, at most, adulterated with nothing more than water. In a highball, of course, the latter was aerated. The average Whiskey drinker regarded the mixture of good Bourbon or Rye with anything as a sort of sacrilege—except after the drink had gone down, when, as a rule, he liked to dispatch a small quantity of water in its wake. To many persons, Whiskey cocktails were so much medicine. To such, the ideal combination was Gin and Vermouth. Vermouth alone, as a drink, never won wide favor in this country, but it is noteworthy that more than half the cocktails known had Vermouth as an essential. Of them all, the favorite was the Dry Martini.

Undoubtedly the ancestor of the cocktail that gained widest vogue during prohibition, particularly among householders who had to make their own, was what was known both as the Adirondack and the Orange Blossom No. 2. It consisted of one-half Orange Juice and one-half Gin, and was served in a bar glass. In the period just past, many persons who thought they had dependable bootleggers made up a concoction that approached the Orange Blossom No. 1, which consisted of one-third Orange Juice, one-third Tom Gin and one-third Italian Vermouth; or else the Eddy, which was one-third Gordon Gin, one-third French Vermouth and one-third Orange Juice. When one's host served a Bronx, during the late Doubtful Drink Era, it was more apt to be something whose content was one of the three just named—or almost anything. As a rule, the Orange Juice, at least, was the "real stuff."

At this point it may be mentioned that between certain pairs of cocktails, the only difference lies in the brand of Gin used. Occasionally the only dissimilarity is in names. However, Shakespeare to the contrary, once in a while there was something in these, as will be shown later.

Despite a widely accepted belief that all cocktails were iced, there were exceptions to the general rule, as the recipes show. My personal preference is for an iced cocktail, and I always use a shaker, one that could hold much more than the quantity of ingredients used. To my notion, a good deal of muscle action is necessary in shaking properly, and one secret of a perfect cocktail is getting it to the drinker with the least possible delay; that is to say, like hot coffee, as soon as it is made.

Just where cocktails leave off and other mixed drinks begin it is difficult to determine. Some authorities would make cocktails all mixed drinks which have to be shaken— and cause dissensions. In reproducing the Old Waldorf Bar Book, I have followed in the main the classification of cocktails therein made. Many other mixed drinks fall into groups—determined, as a rule, by one or more of the ingredients used, or the method of making. Others can not be classified, and so are just listed alphabetically.

Before closing this dissertation on the products of the American School of Drinking, one must say frankly that so far as chemistry and logic are concerned, it would seem that either has had little to do with the formulas of most cocktails. The American School of Drinking, as it existed in other days, was never that of France; and so far as anybody has revealed, the rules of chemistry were never considered in arriving at formulas, nor was any dietitian consulted. Most American alcoholic concoctions exhibit little regard for chemistry, either in theory or application. In France, as Julian Street intimates in his "Wines," recently published, the art of drinking has, in a sense, been guided partly by the laws of chemical reactions. Generations of experts have determined which wines go best with certain foods; which aid the appetite or digestion. Moderation has usually been the keynote.

Americans, as a rule, drink partly for the taste, mostly for the effect. Those who prefer the effect to the taste like to get the same quickly. The cocktail, taken according to general practice, is not sipped as is wine. If it is not gulped, it is usually finished in three swallows, or at most four. Few of us on this side of the Atlantic, when we face a cocktail, look for bouquets or aromas, to a French gourmet among the most potent charms of wines and brandies. Lots of Americans these days seem to like cocktails made of two or more kinds of liqueurs. Such mixtures would tend to shock the sophisticated foreigner, who has been taught that anything of the nature of a liqueur should follow rather than precede a meal. Most American women who acquired the cocktail habit while John Barleycorn was doing time, judging from what one has seen in foreign parts, prefer cocktails that are sweet, even if they are strong. Indeed, during that now happily ended chapter of American history, cocktail parties, which grew into great vogue, were seldom intended to quicken the appetite for dinner. They became occasions when intensive drinking was done and a provident host or hostess, aware that hunger was bound to ensue, prided himself or herself upon furnishing an abundant supply of *hors d'œuvres*, or, as these came themselves to be known, "appetizers;" the result often being that persons who attended cocktail parties preceding dinners so gorged themselves with these "delicate" but nevertheless substantial offerings, that by the time they reached the dinner table they seldom had any appetite left.

Moderation is the secret of enjoyment of anything, if one wishes to retain the faculty for enjoyment. That rule most certainly applies to cocktails and the whole category of drink of any kind. And, according to very respectable doctors, just as many digestive troubles originate from over-eating as from too much drinking.

III. BAPTISMAL

THE visitor to a speakeasy, during the recent Period of Stress, may have lacked nothing in abundance of supply; but he was confronted by decided circumscription in variety. Had one who knew breathed to dispensers of dreadful drinks that masked under names once guarantees of superior content, and harmless, if potent, accelerators of appetite and good feeling—taken in moderation—some figures as well as facts about the quality and variety of alcoholic dispensation at the Old Waldorf in its real prime, he would probably have been greeted by a scouting or scornful, "Aw, what are ya givin' me?" Indeed, had you told almost anybody who hadn't the facts before him the number of kinds of fancy drinks Old Waldorf barmen knew how to concoct, and did concoct, they would have put you down as a liar and probably said it aloud.

Those three hundred or so varieties of what was once the great American drink, one which carried the name of our people all over the world; those over four hundred more varieties of picklers than the most ambitious American pickler of his age was ever able to advertise—and which pickled more people—deserve, with their formulas, to live in history. Their nomenclature belongs to it, not only as part of our national chronicles, but as an index to certain social, industrial and artistic achievements of an age.

Brushing aside such mythological, ornithological, theological, zoological, or otherwise "logical" designations as Adonis, Bird, Bridal, Bishop Poker, Creole, Goat's Delight, Gloom Lifter and Hoptoad—to name just a few samples of cocktails of other times—consider others that betray less of fancy and originality, but perhaps more of cause of origin.

For example, take the Armour, called after a well known Chicago patron of the establishment. Then there was a Beadleston, named after another customer who sold the Bar much of the beer he brewed, and after whom was baptized a second cocktail, the Beadleston No. 2. Speaking still alphabetically, there was a Bunyan, spelled with an "a," not an "o," and summoning up thoughts of a thirsty pilgrim's progress to a land of never-never-thirst. A "Chauncey" must have been named after the most distinguished person of that prenomen, a famous orator and wit. There is no record that its namesake was present at its christening. Nor is there evidence that the originator of a celebrated march upon Washington graced the birth of the Coxey cocktail. The Dorflinger got its name from a glass manufacturer who made containers for drinks.

For the creation of the Eddy, I may predicate at once that no scientific lady of that name was responsible; I am inclined to attribute its origin to a popular and handsome young diplomatist of the early part of the century who married an heiress and went into eclipse. And surely one would not think of attributing the Hearst cocktail to any personal interest on the part of a great newspaper proprietor; rather to certain of his staff who were in the habit of dropping in at odd times when assigned to a story in the neighborhood of what was then Herald Square.

And there was McKinley's Delight. Just why it was

McKinley's delight, I am unable to ascertain. The chances are that President McKinley never found out whether it was or not. In its favor, I may mention that the Bar was a great hangout for the G.O.P.'s of yesteryear, who may have passed their enthusiasm for their candidates across the counter for the barman to translate into terms of liquid intensity.

The Waldorf Bar served a Racquet Club, a Riding Club and a Union League Club cocktail, thus honoring certain social and representative New York institutions. But who the "Mrs. Thompson" was, whose name was bestowed upon one of its cocktails, frankly, I do not know. Nor do I know just what state of spiritual or spirituous elevation, or on whose part, suggested the christening of the St. Francis or the St. Peter or the St. John, though the first may have been called after a California hotel, and not after a friar long deceased.

The stage, whether or not it drove men to drink in those days, certainly inspired much drinking, and successful plays often stood godfather for bartenders' conceptions. The great success of "Rosemary," with which John Drew and one of Charles Frohman's best companies helped open the Astoria part of the Old Waldorf-Astoria, was celebrated in a cocktail of the same name, composed of equal parts of Vermouth and Bourbon. The tuneful "Merry Widow" and the almost equally whistleable "Chocolate Soldier" were drowned in baptismal cocktails at the Waldorf Bar. The Merry Widow cocktail was made of half French Vermouth and half Dubonnet; the Chocolate Soldier, an appropriately stronger potation, was composed of one-third Dubonnet, two-thirds Nicholson Gin and a dash of Lime Juice. "Peg o' My Heart" and "Rob Roy" named other cocktails. "Trilby" had been drunk back in the days of the Waldorf sit-down Bar. In compliment to the locale of the play, the Trilby cocktail was made of one-third French Vermouth and two-thirds Old Tom Gin, with dashes of Orange Bitters and Crème Yvette. "Salomé," making a tremendous sensation in a single presentation at the Metropolitan Opera House, in 1907, was celebrated in a way that might have made Strauss weep for his seidel or his stein of Pilsner. With its two dashes of Absinthe, cementing half portions of Italian Vermouth and Dubonnet, the cocktail lacked German authorship, but certainly nothing in authority. Mrs. Leslie Carter must have heard, when she helped make David Belasco loom larger on the theatrical map, that "Zaza" made one of its biggest hits in the form of an invention of a Waldorf barman. The Zaza cocktail was somewhat milder than the Salomé, for only one-third of its content was Old Tom Gin, that being allied with two-thirds Dubonnet and two dashes of Orange Bitters. And Charlie Chaplin had a cocktail named in his honor when he began to make the screen public laugh.

In those days every big or spectacular event claimed its appropriate honorification at the hands of those Waldorf dispensers of drink. For example, the first composition of the Arctic cocktail celebrated Peary's discovery of the North Pole—or where it ought to be; the Doctor Cook cocktail proclaimed the exposure of a celebrated polar faker whose very entrails Peary once confessed to me personally, in effect, he hated; the invention of the Coronation cocktail was anticipative of the ten minutes' rest the late King Edward got when they sat him on the Stone of Scone. The Fin de Siècle came toward the end

of the century, when the expression became current in
magazines and newspapers, and when lots of Americans
were taking their first steps in French. What they said
when they meant to order such a cocktail is another matter.

Why, you can date many American historical, society,
sporting, police and other events by those cocktails when
you know the names. There was the Third Degree, invented when everybody in New York was interested in the
way tough cops were extracting information from accused
persons. Probably it left its imbiber in a state similar to
that of the victim of a police inquisition. Added to one-
eighth French Vermouth, it consisted of seven-eighths
Plymouth Gin, with several dashes of Absinthe. The Good
Times cocktail was reminiscent of the socially important
coach that once ran from the Waldorf doorway to the
Woodmansten Inn. The Jitney complimented an invention of a Detroit gentleman which was found adaptable
to take the place of trolley cars when drivers and con-
ductors went on strike. It may be particularly interesting
to that inventor to learn that it was composed of one-half
Gin, one-fourth Lemon, one-fourth Orange Juice—and a
little Sugar. Then there was the Marconi Wireless, which
first "materialized" at the Bar of the Old Waldorf when
the ancestor of what is now called the "radio" began to
raise its ghostly voice; and the Prince Henry, concocted
to celebrate the arrival of the once-distinguished Kaiser's
apostolic brother, who was dined and wined prodigiously
in the old hotel's Grand Ballroom, just above the Barroom.

Cocktails by the names of Futurity, Suburban, and so
on, celebrated the triumphs of James R. Keene and his
racing cohorts and other famous stable-owners on near-by

courses. A famous picture of a naked girl in the waves, sold under the name of "September Morn," was perpetuated—at least it was so thought—by a Waldorf cocktail. However, that cocktail was not a brand-new composition —simply a Clover Club cocktail in which Gin gave place to Bacardi Rum; the real Clover Club being composed of the juice of half a Lemon, half a teaspoonful of Sugar, half a pony of Raspberry Syrup, one-quarter pony of White of Egg, and a jigger of Gin.

The Spanish-American War produced distinctive drink nomenclature. The guns of Santiago awakened reverberation in the Waldorf Bar, and shook up what was termed a Santiago Sour—not, however, strictly a cocktail; no more was Hobson's Kiss, reminiscent of an episode that, alas! served to discredit the hero of the *Merrimac*. Then there was a Schley punch, a Shafter cocktail, and another which took its name from Admiral Dewey, victor at Manila Bay.

And when these are named, one has not really begun on the list of appetizers available to those who resorted at regular times to what was long the most famous expositor of the American School of Drinking. As I have said, their nomenclature deserves to live in history, of which it is a part. More, if only to clarify that portion of history with data furnishing contributory evidence—if further proof is impossible—their composition is important to the historian, and some day will so prove to the antiquarian, who will no doubt find material for study and zealous contemplation, if not amazement, in the fact that men once were able, year after year, to get outside so many kinds of more or less ardent spirit, and in such quantity, and still survive.

Well, they didn't all survive. They made patients for the specialists at Carlsbad and other European cure resorts, and in many cases quit this sphere when still in their prime. But when all is said, the searcher for prehistoric man, for ancestors of much greater stature, may halt when he reads of the exploits of the exponents of the old American School of Drinking, point to the record, scratch his head, and say: "There were giants in those days." And others, of course, will draw a moral.

A.

DRUNK AT THE OLD WALDORF BAR

FOR the convenience of students of the cultural history and *mores* of the American people, as well as for those who wish to set a goal before starting to mix, the bibulous concoctions long known and served at the Bar of the Old Waldorf have been arranged alphabetically, and in two general classes. The cocktails have been set down in one list and the others, which might be classed as "beverages," though that title might be open to dispute, have been termed "Fancy Potations and Otherwise." The latter, as already indicated, have themselves been subdivided into "families" bearing a sort of generic name. However, a great many proved too individualistic to classify, and these are merely run alphabetically.

At the Old Waldorf-Astoria Bar a good many non-alcoholic drinks were made and served, and their recipes are included in a separate list.

For the guidance, particularly, of those faced by bottles of authentic liquors and liquids more or less potent and potable, and who may not know just what to do with them, I have separated names of the cocktails contained in the Old Waldorf Bar Book into lists, governed by the particular "base" on which each was made. Many duplications of names will be discovered, but they are intentional, and due to the fact that some cocktails had more than one base.

In addition is given a list of cocktails in which Vermouth

27

is used. In a few it formed the base, or one of the bases. Another table names the cocktails in which Absinthe was considered essential. These lists apply only to the cocktails known and served before the Noble Experiment was launched, and not to "Fancy Potations and Otherwise," of the same period, which have been divided, when possible, into groups according to their general name, such as "Slings," "Sours," "Punches," and so on. Further on in the book will be found the best list, with formulas, of worth-while cocktails, punches and so on, such as Americans going to the Tropics and elsewhere abroad have learned to know and usually to esteem, particularly those based upon two of the best known varieties of Rum produced in the West Indies.

LISTS OF PRE-WAR COCKTAILS BY BASES

ON A GIN BASE

Adirondack	Brandy	Cooperstown
Alaska	Bridal	Cornell
Alexander	Brighton	Coxey
All Right	Bronx	Criss Racquet Club
Alphonse	Bronx No. 2	Daniel de Rouge
Ampersand	Original Bronx	Defender
Amsterdam	Bunyan	Delatour
Astor	Chanler	Delmonico
Astoria	Chanticleer	Dewey
Baco	Chauncey	Dr. Cook
Ballantine	Chocolate Soldier	Dorflinger
Bishop Poker	Christ	Dorlando
Black	Clover Club	Dowd
Blackthorn	Club	Down
Bradford	Colonial	Easy

Eddy
Emerson
Fin de Siècle
Fourth Degree
Gibson
Gibson No. 2
Gin
Gladwin
Gold
Good Times
Grand Vin
Guion
Hall
Halsey
Hamlin
Hearst
Hilliard
Holland Gin
Honolulu
Honolulu No. 3
Howard
Ideal
I. D. K.
I. D. K. No. 2
James
Jazz
Jimmie Lee
Jitney
Jockey Club
Johnson
Lewis
Lone Tree
Love
Lynne
MacLean

Marble Hill
Marguerite
Marmalade
Martini
Dry Martini
Middleton
Milliken
Millionaire
Milo
Montauk
Mrs. Thompson
My Own
Newman
Newport
Number Three
Nutting
Oliver
Opal
Orange Blossom
Orange Blossom
   No. 2
Passipe
Pell
Perfect
Perfect No. 2
Poet's Dream
Pomeroy
Porto Rico
Prince Henry
Princeton
Queen
Racquet Club
Rees
Rose
Rossington

Rossington No. 2
St. Francis
St. John
St. Peter
Shafter
Shake-up-Silo
Silver
Sir Jasper
Skipper
Sloe Gin
Somerset
Soul Kiss
Sunshine
Swan
Tango
Thanksgiving
Third Degree
Three-to-One
Tom Gin
Trilby
Turf
Tuxedo
Union League
Vandervere
Van Wyck
Wall Street
Walter Monteith
West India
White Elephant
H. P. Whitney
Widow
Wild Cherry
Yale
Zaza
1915

ON A WHISKEY BASE

(B. indicates Bourbon; S., Scotch; I., Irish; otherwise Rye was used)

Amaranth
Beadleston
Beadleston No. 2
  (S.)
Brown
Chauncey
Commodore No. 2
  (B.)
Emerald (I.)
Ewing
Express (S.)
Fanciulli
Gloom Lifter (I.)
Hearn's
Highland (S.)
Honolulu No. 2

Japalac
Liberal
Manhattan
Manhattan Junior
Manhattan Punch
McKinley's Delight
Narragansett
Old Fashioned
  Whiskey (B. or
  Rye)
Pan American
Prince
Robert Burns (S.)
Robin (S.)
Rob Roy (S.)
Rory O'More (I.)

Rosemary (B.)
Sazerac (B. or S.)
Sherman
Southgate
Suburban
Thompson
Waldorf
Waldorf Gloom
  Lifter (I.)
Whiskey (B., S., I.
  or Rye)
Whiskey Old Style
  (B. or Rye)
York (S.)

ON A BRANDY OR A LIQUEUR BASE

(B. indicates Brandy. See also "Drinks from Other Climes")

Alaska (Chartreuse)
Alexander (Crème
  de Cacao)
Alphonse (Crème de
  Cacao)
Ampersand (B.)
Bijou (Grand Mar-
  nier)
Bird (B. and Cura-
  çao)
Brandy (B.)
Brandy Crusta (B.)
Brant (B. & White
  Mint)

Charlie Rose (B.)
Chauncey (B.)
Chocolate
  (Chartreuse and
  Maraschino)
Coffee (B.)
Commodore No. 2
  (Crème de Cacao)
Coronation
  (Apricot Brandy)
Fanciulli (Fernet
  Branca)
Floater (B. and
  Kümmel)

Full House
  (Chartreuse and
  Benedictine)
Goat's Delight
  (B. and Kirsch-
  wasser)
Harvard (B.)
Honolulu No. 3
  (Curaçao)
Hop Frog (B.)
Hop Toad (Apricot
  Brandy)
Jack Rose (Grena-
  dine)

Japanese (B.)
Metropole (B.)
Middleton (Grenadine)
Montana (B.)
Netherland (B. and Curaçao)
Peacock (B.)
Peplo (7 Bases, *q.v.*)
Poet's Dream (Benedictine)
Rose (Grand Marnier)
Ruby (Cherry Brandy)
Russian (B.)
Sam Ward (Chartreuse)
Skipper (Maraschino)
Stephen's (Benedictine)
Strawberry (B.)
Tango No. 2 (Benedictine)
Three-to-One (Apricot Brandy)
Waldorf-Astoria (Benedictine)
Woxum (Chartreuse)
"1915" (Curaçao)

ON A RUM BASE

(*For many other Rum Cocktails, see "Drinks from Other Climes"*)

Bacardi
Bacardi No. 2
Commodore
Cora Middleton
Hop Toad
Middleton
Palmetto
Peg o' My Heart
Polo
Raleigh
Santiago
September Morn
Suburban
Tango No. 2

ON A SLOE GIN BASE

Arctic
Ardsley
Bradford
Charlie Chaplin
Futurity
Ping Pong
Porto Rico
Sloe Gin
Tipperary
Tyrone
Van Wyck

ON A BASE OF APPLE WHISKEY, APPLE BRANDY, APPLEJACK, OR "JERSEY LIGHTNING"

Coronation (Applejack)
Full House (Apple Whiskey)
Jack Rose (Applejack)
Jersey (Apple Whiskey)
Marconi Wireless (Applejack)
Normandie (Apple Whiskey)
Star (Apple Whiskey)

IN WHICH IS CALISAYA

Arctic	Colonial	Riding Club
Ardsley	Daniel de Rouge	Robin
Brut	Dorando	
Calisaya	James	

WITH DUBONNET

Chocolate Soldier	Merry Widow	Zaza
Marble Hill	Salomé	

WITH SHERRY

Adonis	Bamboo	Tuxedo
Armour	Stephen's	

WITH PORT

Coffee	Suburban	Union League

WITH SWEDISH PUNSCH

Astor	Doctor

COCKTAILS IN WHICH ABSINTHE IS USED

Absinthe	Goat's Delight	Russian
Ballantine	Hearn's	Salomé
Brut	Loftus	Sazerac
Creole	McKinley's Delight	Sherman
Crook	Opal	Swan
Dorflinger	Peacock	Third Degree
Duchess	Pick-Me-Up	Vivary
Duke	Rees	Waldorf
Fourth Degree	Robert Burns	

IN WHICH VERMOUTH IS USED

Adonis	Defender	Ideal
All Right	Delatour	I. D. K.
Ampersand	Delmonico	I. D. K. No. 2
Amsterdam	Dewey	Japalac
Armour	Dowd	Jazz
Astoria	Down	Jimmie Lee
Baco	Duchess	Johnson
Ballantine	Duke	Lewis
Bamboo	Duplex	Liberal
Beadleston	Easy	Lieut. Colonel
Beadleston No. 2	Eddy	Loftus
Bijou	Emerald	Lone Tree
Bishop Poker	Emerson	Love
Black	Express	Lynne
Blackthorn	Fanciulli	MacLean
Bradford	Fin de Siècle	Manhattan
Bridal	Florida	Manhattan Junior
Brighton	Fourth Degree	Manhattan Punch
Bronx	Futurity	Marconi Wireless
Bronx No. 2	Gibson	Marguerite
Original Bronx	Gibson No. 2	Marmalade
Brown	Gladwin	Martini
Brut	Good Times	Dry Martini
Chanler	Gold	McKinley's Delight
Chanticleer	Grand Vin	Merry Widow
Chauncey	Guion	Metropole
Christ	Hall	Metropolitan
Club	Halsey	Milliken
Cooperstown	Hamlin	Millionaire
Cornell	Harvard	Milo
Coronation	Hearn's	Montauk
Coxey	Hearst	Mrs. Thompson
Creole	Highland	My Own
Criss Racquet Club	Hilliard	Narragansett
Crook	Honolulu No. 2	Neudine

Newman	Rory O'More	Third Degree
New Orleans	Rosemary	Thompson
Newport	Rossington	Tipperary
Normandie	Rossington No. 2	Tip Top
Number Three	Ruby	Trilby
Nutting	St. Francis	Turf
Olivet	St. John	Tyrone
Opal	Salomé	Vandervere
Orange Blossom	Sazerac	Vermouth (French)
Palmetto	Shafter	Vermouth (Italian)
Passipe	Shake-up Silo	Vin Mariani
Pell	Sherman	Vivary
Perfect	Silver	Waldorf
Perfect No. 2	Sir Jasper	Wall Street
Pick-Me-Up	Somerset	Walter Monteith
Poet's Dream	Soul Kiss	West India
Pomeroy	Star	White Elephant
Prince Henry	Stephen's	H. P. Whitney
Queen	Sunshine	Whittaker
Racquet Club	Swan	Widow
Rees	Tango	Woxum
Robert Burns	Tango No. 2	Yale
Rob Roy	Thanksgiving	York

COCKTAILS *

GENERAL DIRECTION: The best method of making most cocktails is to put the ingredients into a shaker in the order named in the recipe; then add cracked ice; then shake vigorously and long; then strain the contents into the cocktail glass and serve promptly. Certain recipes, however, call for "stirring." These are marked "(Stir)," usually on the last line of the formula. Shaking makes a weaker drink.

* Explanation or exposition of names of recipes starred has been given earlier in the book. No effort has been made to compile an encyclopedia, the author believing that research specialists interested in American *mores* would appreciate being left a little wet virgin territory of their own.

ABSINTHE   Two dashes of Gin
                  Two-thirds Absinthe
                  One-third Water (Stir)

ADIRONDACK   One-half Orange Juice
               One-half Gordon Gin
    Rugged, like its namesake. So rugged, indeed, it survived through the prohibition stress and, except that the "gin" might be almost anything else, was one of the few cocktail recipes widely known and followed in this country. But most who made it and drank it did not know its original name!

ADONIS   Two dashes Orange Bitters
                One-half Sherry
                One-half Italian Vermouth (Stir)
    Named in honor of a theatrical offering which first made Henry E. Dixey and Fanny Ward famous.

ALASKA   Dash of Orange Bitters
                One-third Yellow Chartreuse
                Two-thirds Tom Gin

ALEXANDER   One-third Gin
                One-third Crème de Cacao
                One-third Cream

ALL RIGHT   One-fifth Italian Vermouth
                Four-fifths Nicholson Gin
                Piece of Orange Peel in Glass

ALPHONSE   One-third Crème de Cacao
                One-third Dry Gin
                One-third Cream (no ice)

A cartoonist created a series of newspaper comics some thirty years ago, based upon traditional French politeness. "After you, my dear Gaston," "After you, my dear Alphonse," was the text or tenor of the captions.

AMARANTH   One dash Angostura Bitters
              Two-thirds jigger Whiskey
              Stir; fill from siphon; add powdered
              Sugar

AMMONIA   Five drops Aromatic Spirits Ammonia
              One jigger Water (Stir)
      Considered a cure, rather than a cause.

AMPERSAND   Two dashes Orange Bitters
              One-third Brandy
              One-third Tom Gin
              One-third Italian Vermouth
              Two dashes of Curaçao on top

AMSTERDAM   One-third   Vermouth   (French   or
              Italian)
              Dash Orange Bitters
              Two-thirds Nicholson's Gin (Stir)
              Lemon Peel, squeezed on top

ARCTIC *   Dash of Orange Bitters
              One-half Red Calisaya Bark
              One-half Sloe Gin (Stir)

ARDSLEY   Dash of Orange Bitters
              One-half Red Calisaya
              One-half Sloe Gin
      Residents of a famous and wealthy community up the

Hudson, by that name, furnished a good deal of patronage to the Bar.

ARMOUR *   Two dashes Orange Bitters
One-half jigger Sherry
One-half jigger Italian Vermouth (Stir)

ASTOR   One dash of Lemon Juice
One dash of Orange Juice
One jigger of Gin
One jigger of Swedish Punsch (Stir)

Perhaps after William Waldorf, who built the original Waldorf. However, chances are, it was originated either at the old Astor House or the Astor Hotel, and took its name from its bar of nativity.

ASTORIA   Two dashes Orange Bitters
One-third Tom Gin
Two-thirds French Vermouth (Stir)

After the big annex to the old Waldorf, which at its opening, in 1897, became the main part of the establishment.

BACARDI   Two jiggers Bacardi Rum
Two Limes
A little Sugar
A little Grenadine

BACARDI   Juice of one Lime
No. 2   One-half spoonful Sugar
A drink of Bacardi Rum
A little Pineapple Juice
Champagne glass, with shaved Ice

BACO
Dash of Orange Bitters
One-quarter Italian Vermouth
One-quarter French Vermouth
One-half Gordon Gin (Stir)
Slice of Orange Peel, whiskey glass

BALLANTINE
Two dashes Orange Bitters
One-half jigger French Vermouth
One-half jigger Plymouth Gin
One dash Absinthe

BAMBOO
Two dashes Orange Bitters
One-half Sherry
One-half French Vermouth (Stir)

BEADLESTON * Two dashes Orange Bitters
One-half jigger French Vermouth
One-half jigger Whiskey (Stir)

BEADLESTON
No. 2 *
One-half French Vermouth
One-half Haig & Haig Scotch Whiskey

BIJOU
Two dashes Orange Bitters
One-half French Vermouth
One-half Grand Marnier (Stir)

BIRD
Twist two pieces Orange Peel
Fill glass with fine Ice
Two-thirds Triple Sec Curaçao
One-third Brandy
Two more Twisted Orange Peels
Serve as Crème de Menthe Frappé

So named by the person on whom it was first tried.
"That's a bird!" he exclaimed, smacking his lips.

BISHOP One-third French Vermouth
POKER One-third Italian Vermouth
One-third Plymouth Gin
Dash of Amer Picon Bitters

BLACK Two-thirds Italian Vermouth
One-third Tom Gin

BLACK- One pony Kirschwasser
JACK One dash Brandy
One pony Coffee (claret glass)
Supposed to have been called that from knockout effects consequent upon indulgence.

BLACK- Two dashes Orange Bitters
THORN One-third Italian Vermouth
Two-thirds Sloe Gin (Stir)
Sloe Gin, a distillation of the fruit of the blackthorn, gave authority to the drink and to its derivation as well.

BRADFORD Two dashes Orange Bitters
One-half Italian Vermouth
One-half Tom Gin
Twist Lemon Peel on top

BRANDY One dash Angostura Bitters
One dash Gin
One jigger Brandy (Stir)

BRANDY One-half Brandy or Applejack
No. 2 One-half French Vermouth
One dash Orange Bitters

BRANDY   Cup one-half small Lemon
CRUSTA   Put in cocktail glass
             Dip edge of glass in powdered Sugar
             In mixing glass put two dashes Angostura
                 Bitters
             Four drops Lemon Juice
             Two dashes Curaçao
             Jigger Brandy (Stir and pour)

BRANT   Two dashes Angostura Bitters
             One-quarter White Mint
             Three-quarters Brandy (Stir)
             Piece of Lemon Peel on top

BRIDAL   Two dashes Orange Bitters
             Dash of Maraschino
             One-third jigger Italian Vermouth
             Two-thirds jigger Plymouth Gin (Stir)
             Piece of Orange Peel, twisted, in glass

BRIGHTON Dash of Orange Bitters
             One-half Tom Gin
             One-half Italian Vermouth (Stir)
     So called from the race course near Brighton Beach,
where many Bar habitués spent their afternoons when
that track topped the racing calendar.

BRONX   One-fourth Italian Vermouth
             One-fourth French Vermouth
             One-half Gordon Gin
             Piece of Orange Peel

BRONX No. 2	Two jiggers Gin
	One jigger French Vermouth
	One-half jigger Orange Juice

BRONX (WAL-DORF)	Two-thirds Gin
	One-third Orange Juice
	Two slices fresh Pineapple in glass

BRONX (Original)	One-third Orange Juice
	Two-thirds Gin
	Dash of French Vermouth
	Dash of Italian Vermouth

Many claimants to the honor of inventing the Bronx have arisen. It was an Old Waldorf tradition that the inventor was Johnnie Solon (or Solan), popular as one of the best mixers behind its bar counter for most of the latter's history. This is Solon's own story of the Creation—of the Bronx:

"We had a cocktail in those days called the Duplex, which had a pretty fair demand. One day, I was making one for a customer when in came Traverson, head waiter of the Empire Room—the main dining room in the original Waldorf. A Duplex was composed of equal parts of French and Italian Vermouth, shaken up with squeezed orange peel, or two dashes of Orange Bitters. Traverson said, 'Why don't you get up a new cocktail? I have a customer who says you can't do it.'

" 'Can't I?' I replied.

"Well, I finished the Duplex I was making, and a thought came to me. I poured into a mixing glass the equivalent of two jiggers of Gordon Gin. Then I filled the jigger with orange juice, so that it made one-third of orange juice and two-thirds of Gin. Then into the mixture I put a dash each of Italian and French Vermouth, shaking the thing up. I didn't taste it myself, but I poured it into a cocktail glass and handed it to Traverson and said: 'You are a pretty good judge. (He was.) See what you think of that.' Traverson tasted it. Then he swallowed it whole.

" 'By God!' he said, 'you've really got something new! That will make a big hit. Make me another and I will take it back to that customer in the dining room. Bet you'll sell a lot of them. Have you got plenty of oranges? If you haven't, you better stock up, because I'm going to sell a lot of those cocktails during lunch.'

"The demand for Bronx cocktails started that day. Pretty soon we were using a whole case of oranges a day. And then several cases.

"The name? No, it wasn't really named directly after the borough or the river so-called. I had been at the Bronx Zoo a day or two before, and I saw, of course, a lot of beasts I had never known. Customers used to tell me of the strange animals they saw after a lot of mixed drinks. So when Traverson said to me, as he started to take the drink in to the customer, 'What'll I tell him is the name of this drink?' I thought of those animals, and said: 'Oh, you can tell him it is a "Bronx." ' "

BROWN   Two dashes Orange Bitters
          One-half French Vermouth
          One-half Whiskey

Ascribed to students of Brown University, an early Rockefeller Center.

BRUT   Two dashes Orange Bitters
            One-half French Vermouth
            One-half Calisaya
            One dash Absinthe
An extremely "dry" cocktail. "Brut" (French) means "raw." Many customers pronounced it "Brute," and so thought it.

BUNYAN *   Gordon Gin
            One Olive
            Carbonic on side

CALISAYA   Two dashes Orange Bitters
            One jigger Calisaya (Stir)

CHAMPAGNE   One lump Sugar
            Two dashes Angostura Bitters
            One piece Lemon Peel, twisted
            Fill glass with chilled Champagne

CHANLER   One small piece of Ice in mixing glass
            Squeeze one piece of Lemon Peel
            One-third Italian Vermouth
            Two-thirds Old Tom Gin (whiskey
                glass)
"Sheriff Bob" Chanler, artist, married Lina Cavalieri, of the Metropolitan and made the front pages early in the century.

CHANTICLEER One-half Orange Gin
            One-half French Vermouth
            White of one Egg
            (Add a Cock's Comb if desired)

Celebrated the local opening of Edmond Rostand's *Chanticler*.

CHARLIE
CHAPLIN
    One-third Lime Juice
One-third Sloe Gin
One-third Apricot Brandy

CHARLIE
ROSE
    One pony Brandy
Slice of Lemon placed on top (no Ice)

CHAUNCEY *
    Dash of Orange Bitters
One-fourth Tom Gin
One-fourth Whiskey
One-fourth Italian Vermouth
One-fourth Brandy (Stir)

CHOCOLATE
    One pony yellow Chartreuse
One pony Maraschino
Yolk of one Egg (claret glass)

CHOCOLATE
SOLDIER *
    One-third Dubonnet
Two-thirds Nicholson's Gin
Dash of Lime Juice

CHRIST
    Two dashes Orange Bitters
One-half Plymouth Gin
One-half Italian Vermouth
Two slices Orange Peel

CIDER
    Two dashes Angostura Bitters
Whole Lemon Peel
One lump Ice in Collins glass
One pint Cider (Stir)

CLIQUET   Juice one Orange
One jigger Rye; flavored with St.
    Croix Rum
One lump Ice (Stir)

CLOVER CLUB Juice one-half Lemon
One-half spoon Sugar
One-half pony Raspberry Syrup
One-fourth pony White of Egg
One jigger Gin (star glass)

A Philadelphia importation, originated in the bar of the old Bellevue-Stratford, where the Clover Club, composed of literary, legal, financial and business lights of the Quaker City, often dined and wined, and wined again.

CLUB   Dash of Angostura Bitters
One-third Italian Vermouth
Two-thirds Plymouth Gin (Stir)

COFFEE   Two ponies Port Wine
One pony Brandy
Yolk of one Egg
One-half spoon Sugar (claret glass)

COLONIAL   Dash of Orange Bitters
Two-thirds Plymouth Gin
One-third Red Calisaya (Stir)

COMMODORE One-half teaspoon Sugar
One dash Lemon Juice
White of one Egg
One drink of Bacardi Rum

	One dash of Grenadine One dash of Raspberry Syrup
COMMODORE No. 2	One-third Lemon Juice One-third Bourbon Whiskey One-third Crème de Cacao Dash Grenadine Syrup (champagne glass)
COOPERSTOWN	Bronx, with fresh Mint
CORA MIDDLETON	Clover Club made with Jamaica Rum instead of Gin (claret glass)
CORNELL	One-half French Vermouth One-half Gordon Gin

A compliment to an institution at Ithaca, many of whose alumni—mining engineers and others—used it to toast Alma Mater.

CORONATION *	One-third Italian Vermouth One-third French Vermouth One-third Applejack One dash Apricot Brandy
COXEY *	Dash of Amer Picon Bitters One-half Italian Vermouth One-half Plymouth Gin (Stir)
CREOLE	Dash of Orange Bitters One-third jigger Absinthe One-third jigger Italian Vermouth
CRISS RACQUET CLUB	Dash of Orange Bitters One-half French Vermouth

One-half Plymouth Gin
Frappé with Orange Peel

CROOK   Dash of Orange Bitters
One-third Absinthe
Two-thirds Italian Vermouth

DANIEL   Orange Bitters
DE ROUGE   One-half Tom Gin
One-half Red Calisaya (Stir)

DEFENDER   Dash of Orange Bitters
One-half Tom Gin
One-half Italian Vermouth
Two dashes Crème Yvette (Stir)
The name of an American yacht which took care of
one of Sir Thomas Lipton's early but seemingly endless
"Shamrocks."

DELATOUR   One-third Italian Vermouth
Two-thirds Gordon Gin
Two dashes Orange Bitters
Twist Orange Peel in glass

DELMONICO   Dash of Orange Bitters
One-half French Vermouth
One-half Plymouth Gin
Two slices Orange Peel
Adopted from the bar of Old Delmonico's, a long-
famous New York restaurant.

DEWEY *   Dash of Orange Bitters
One-half Plymouth Gin
One-half French Vermouth

DOCTOR   One-half Lime Juice
                  One-half Swedish Punsch

DR. COOK *   Juice one-half Lemon
                  White of one Egg
                  Two dashes Maraschino
                  Three-fourths Gin (claret glass)

DORFLINGER *   Dash of Orange Bitters
                  One-third Green Absinthe
                  Two-thirds Plymouth Gin

DORLANDO   Same as Daniel de Rouge
    After an Italian marathon runner in the Olympic
games in London, 1908.

DOWD   One-half Italian Vermouth
                  One-half Gordon Gin

DOWN   Dash of Orange Bitters
                  One-third Italian Vermouth
                  Two-thirds Gordon Gin (with
                      Olive)
    What else, in faith, than a county in Ireland—ancient
home of many American bartenders?

DUCHESS   Dash of Orange Bitters
                  One-third Absinthe
                  One-third French Vermouth
                  One-third Italian Vermouth

DUKE   Dash of Orange Bitters
                  Two dashes, each of Absinthe and
                      Anisette
                  One jigger French Vermouth

DUPLEX — Two dashes Orange Bitters, or two squeezes of Orange Peel
One-half Italian Vermouth
One-half French Vermouth

EASY — Dash of Orange Bitters
One-eighth Italian Vermouth
Seven-eighths Booth's Gin

EDDY * — One-third Gordon Gin
One-third French Vermouth
One-third Orange Juice

EMERALD — Dash of Orange Bitters
One-half Italian Vermouth
One-half Irish Whiskey (Stir)

EMERSON — Juice one-half Lime
Small teaspoon Maraschino
One-third Italian Vermouth
One-third Tom Gin (Stir)

EWING — One drop Angostura Bitters
One jigger Whiskey (Stir)

EXPRESS — Dash of Orange Bitters
One-half Italian Vermouth
One-half Scotch Whiskey (Stir)

FANCIULLI — One-fourth Fernet Branca
One-fourth Italian Vermouth
One-half Whiskey
Frappé or not. Devotees usually took it without Ice,

FIN DE SIÈCLE *   Orange Bitters
One dash Amer Picon Bitters
One-third Italian Vermouth
Two-thirds Plymouth Gin (Stir)

FLOATER   Fill glass with shaved Ice
Three-fourths Gilka Kümmel
One-fourth Brandy

There is equal authority for a contention that this was called after a racehorse owned by the late James R. Keene, or after an individual numerically important, and who was transported into various precincts at different hours of Election Day and thereby enabled to vote early and often, as the saying was.

FLORIDA   One-half Italian Vermouth
One-half Orange Juice

FOURTH DEGREE   One-third Italian Vermouth
Two-thirds Plymouth Gin
Dash of Absinthe

FULL HOUSE   Dash of Angostura Bitters
One-third Yellow Chartreuse
One-third Benedictine
One-third Apple Whiskey

The name is indicative of the sway once enjoyed by what was the great American indoor game in B.C. days —that is to say Before Contract, or Before Culbertson.

FUTURITY *   Dash of Angostura Bitters
One-half Sloe Gin
One-half Italian Vermouth (Stir)

GIBSON
One-half French Vermouth
One-half Dry Tom Gin (Stir)
Squeeze Lemon Peel on top

GIBSON No. 2
One-third French Vermouth
Two-thirds Plymouth Gin
Orange Peel on top

GIN
Dash of Orange Bitters
One jigger Tom Gin (Stir)

GINGER ALE
One lump Ice
Two dashes Angostura Bitters
One whole Lemon Peel
Fill with cold Ginger Ale

GLADWIN
Three-fourths Gordon Gin
One-eighth Italian Vermouth
One-eighth French Vermouth

GLOOM LIFTER
Same as Clover Club
Irish Whiskey instead of Gin
One-half teaspoon Brandy

GOAT'S DELIGHT
One-half Kirschwasser
One-half Brandy
One dash Orgeat Syrup
One spoon Cream
One dash Absinthe

As to who was the original "goat" cheered by this cup, records are at least vague.

GOLD
Dash of Orange Bitters
One-half Tom Gin
One-half Italian Vermouth

After the product of "them thar hills," finders of which came to the Bar in great numbers.

GOOD TIMES *   Dash of Orange Bitters
                One-third French Vermouth
                Two-thirds Booth's Gin (Stir;
                    Olive)

GRAND VIN   One-fourth Italian Vermouth
                One-fourth French Vermouth
                One-half Plymouth Gin

GUION   Dash of Orange Bitters
                One-half Plymouth Gin
                One-half Italian Vermouth
                One spoon of Benedictine on top
    Called after a member of the family which owned, or had founded, the Guion line of steamships.

HALL   Dash of Orange Bitters
                One-third jigger Italian Vermouth
                One-third French Vermouth
                One-third Nicholson Gin (Olive)

HALSEY   One-half Gordon Gin
                One-fourth Italian Vermouth
                One-fourth French Vermouth
                Squeeze Orange Peel (whiskey glass)
    Named in compliment to a well known stock-broker and patron of the Bar.

HAMLIN   One-third Italian Vermouth
                Two-thirds Nicholson Gin
    Took its name from Harry Hamlin of Buffalo, an

enthusiastic automobilist in the days when there were far more enthusiasts than automobiles.

HARVARD   Dash of Orange Bitters
Two-fifths jigger Brandy
Three-fifths Italian Vermouth (Stir)
Fill from chilled siphon

Named after a school for young men, whose site is contiguous to the Charles River, in a suburb of Boston. Alumni who drank it sometimes lost the "Harvard accent."

HEARN'S   Dash of Manhattan Bitters
One-third Whiskey
One-third Italian Vermouth
One-third Absinthe

HEARST *   One dash Orange Bitters
One dash Angostura Bitters
One-half jigger Italian Vermouth
One-half jigger Plymouth Gin

HIGHLAND   Dash of Orange Bitters
One-half Scotch
One-half Italian Vermouth (Stir)

HILLIARD   Dash of Peychaud Bitters
One-third Italian Vermouth
Two-thirds Dry Gin (Stir)

HOFFMAN   Two dashes Orange Bitters
HOUSE   One-third French Vermouth
Two-thirds Plymouth Gin
Squeeze Lemon Peel on top

Conceived at the old Hotel in Madison Square whose bar was famous before the Old Waldorf was built, for the length of its brass rail, the Bougereau painting of nudities on the wall, and the notability of many of its patrons. Served at Old Waldorf Bar, but was not in the original Bar Book.

HOLLAND GIN	Dash of Angostura Bitters One jigger Holland Gin (Stir)
HONOLULU	Two dashes Angostura Bitters One teaspoon Lime Juice One teaspoon Orange Juice One jigger Tom Gin Twist Lemon Peel on top
HONOLULU No. 2	One-third Italian Vermouth One-third French Vermouth One third Whiskey
HONOLULU No. 3	Two jiggers Gin A little less than half a jigger of 　　Orange Curaçao Juice of half a Lime
HOP FROG	Two-thirds Lime Juice One-third Brandy
HOP TOAD	Juice of one-half Lime One-third Jamaica Rum One-third Apricot Brandy
HOWARD	Dash of Orange Bitters One jigger Plymouth Gin (Stir) Two dashes Angostura Bitters

IDEAL
One-third Italian Vermouth
Two-thirds Plymouth Gin
Flavor with Grapefruit

I. D. K.
One-third Italian Vermouth
Two-thirds Nicholson Gin
Orange Peel (Stir. Bar glass)

I. D. K. No. 2
One-fifth Italian Vermouth
Four-fifths Nicholson Gin
Sprig of Mint

JACK ROSE
(or *Jacque Rose*)
Juice of Lime
One-third Grenadine Syrup
Two-thirds Applejack

So called because of its pink color, the exact shade of a Jacqueminot rose, when properly concocted.

JAMES
Dash of Orange Bitters
Two-thirds Plymouth Gin
One-third Red Calisaya (Stir)

JAPALAC
Juice one-fourth Orange
One jigger French Vermouth
One jigger Whiskey
Dash of Raspberry Syrup

So styled in compliment to a salesman who sold a product of that name; not because it would enamel a digestive apparatus.

JAPANESE
Dash of Boker's Bitters
Two dashes Orgeat Syrup
One jigger Brandy
One slice Lemon Peel (Stir)

JAZZ   Same as Bronx, with plenty of
                  Orange Juice

Commemorating the sudden but widespread popularity of modern rhythmical measures when the century
was still young.

JERSEY   Dash of Boker's Bitters
                  Two dashes Syrup
                  One jigger Apple Whiskey (Stir)

JIMMIE LEE   Dash of Peychaud Bitters
                  One-third French Vermouth
                  One-third Italian Vermouth
                  One-third Plymouth Gin
                  Serve with Orange Peel

JITNEY *   One-half Gin
                  One-quarter Lemon Juice
                  One-fourth Orange Juice
                  A little Sugar

JOCKEY CLUB   Dash of Orange Bitters
                  One jigger Dry Gin (Stir)

Not after the perfume, but after the American Jockey
Club itself.

JOHNSON   Dash of Orange Bitters
                  One-third jigger Plymouth Gin
                  One-third jigger French Vermouth
                  One-third jigger Italian Vermouth
                     (Stir)
                  Piece of Orange Peel on top

LEWIS   One-half French Vermouth
                  One-half Plymouth Gin

Named, not after Sinclair, but before the author of "Main Street" had discovered Broadway.

LIBERAL	Dash of Orange Bitters Three dashes Amer Picon One-half Whiskey One-half Italian Vermouth (Stir)
LIEUTENANT COLONEL	One-half French Vermouth One-half Amer Picon Bitters
LOFTUS	One-third French Vermouth One-third Italian Vermouth One-third Absinthe

Called in compliment to Cissie Loftus, famous English comedienne and mimic, long a popular top-liner.

LONE TREE	Dash of Orange Bitters One-half Italian Vermouth One-half Plymouth Gin

After the 1899 equivalent of a "nineteenth hole"—a tree which stood alone in a secluded part of a golf course near Philadelphia. Players on that course frequented the Old Waldorf Bar.

LOVE	Martini Cocktail, with White of one Egg added
LYNNE	One-half French Vermouth One-half Gordon Gin
MacLEAN	One-quarter Italian Vermouth One-quarter French Vermouth One-half Gordon Gin

In honor of John R. MacLean, long proprietor of the Cincinnati *Enquirer* and the Washington *Post*.

McKINLEY'S   One dash Absinthe
DELIGHT   Two dashes Cherry Brandy
                  Two-thirds Whiskey
                  One-third Italian Vermouth (Stir)

MANHATTAN   Dash of Orange Bitters
                  One-half Italian Vermouth
                  One-half Rye Whiskey (Stir)
                  Serve with Maraschino Cherry

Origin somewhat obscure. Probably first called after a well known club of that name, and not after an island famed for many years as the abode and domain of a certain "Tiger."

MANHATTAN   Two dashes Orange Bitters
No. 2   Two pinches Sugar
                  One-half Italian Vermouth
                  One-half Irish Whiskey

MANHATTAN   One-half Vermouth
JUNIOR   One-half Whiskey
                  Piece of Orange Peel

MANHATTAN   Manhattan cocktail in red ground
PUNCH   glass.—*Editor's Note: Last three
(Waldorf)   words denote a container, not an
                  ingredient.*

MARBLE HILL   One-quarter Dubonnet
                  One-quarter Orange Juice
                  One-half Gordon Gin

MARCONI WIRELESS *	Two dashes Orange Bitters One-third Italian Vermouth Two-thirds Applejack

MARGUERITE	Dash of Orange Bitters One-half French Vermouth One-half Plymouth Gin

MARMALADE	One-quarter French Vermouth One-quarter Italian Vermouth One-half Nicholson Gin Two slices Orange

MARTINI	Dash of Orange Bitters One-half Tom Gin One-half Italian Vermouth (Stir) Serve with a green Olive Twist piece of Lemon Peel on top

MARTINI No. 2	Two jiggers Gin One-half jigger Italian Vermouth One-half jigger French Vermouth (Stir) Serve as above

MARTINI (Dry)	Two-thirds Gin One-third French (or Sec) Vermouth (Stir) Serve as above

MARTINI (Dry No. 2)	One-half Gin (preferably dry) One-half French Vermouth (Stir) Serve as above

Modern practice prescribes shaking for a Dry Martini.

This, however, weakens the mixture and used to be discountenanced by barmen who believed in tradition.

MERRY WIDOW *   One-half French Vermouth
One-half Dubonnet

METROPOLE   One dash Peychaud Bitters
One dash Orange Bitters
One-half French Vermouth
One-half Brandy (Stir; Maraschino Cherry)

Attributed to a once well known and somewhat lively hotel, whose bar was long a center of life after dark in the Times Square district.

METROPOLITAN   Two-thirds Manhattan Bitters
One-third Italian Vermouth (Stir)

After a New York club, long popularly called "The Millionaires'."

MIDDLETON   One-half Jamaica Rum
One-quarter Grenadine Syrup
One-quarter Holland Gin
One White of Egg
Juice of one Lemon

MILLIKEN   Three dashes Amer Picon Bitters
One-quarter French Vermouth
One-quarter Italian Vermouth
One-half Gordon Gin

MILLIONAIRE   Dry Martini, with Grenadine on top

MILO   One-sixth Pomelo Bitters
One-third Italian Vermouth

One-half Plymouth Gin

MONAHAN
SPECIAL

Dash of Amer Picon Bitters
Two-thirds Whiskey
One-third Italian Vermouth (Stir)

Called after Mike Monahan, one of the Waldorf bar-keepers, its inventor.

MONTANA

One-third Brandy
One-third French Vermouth
One-third Port Wine (Stir)

A compliment to the field of operations of many early patrons of the Bar.

MONTAUK

One-third French Vermouth
One-third Italian Vermouth
One-third Gin
Two dashes Peychaud Bitters (Stir)
Serve in "old-fashioned" glass

Named about the time that men of vision began to talk of Montauk Point as the Western terminus of transatlantic steamship lines.

MOUNTAIN

Whiskey glass two-thirds full of Cider
One whole Egg
Pepper and Salt to taste

MRS. THOMPSON

One-third French Vermouth
Two-thirds Gordon Gin

MY OWN

One-half French Vermouth
One-half Plymouth Gin

NARRAGANSETT   One-third Italian Vermouth
Two-thirds Rye Whiskey
One dash Anisette (Stir)

After Narragansett Pier, during the "Nineties" the summer abode of many wealthy patrons of the Old Waldorf Bar.

NETHERLAND   Dash of Orange Bitters
Two-thirds Brandy
One-third Curaçao (Stir)

Possibly invented at the Hotel Netherland, a contemporary of the Old Waldorf.

NEUDINE   Dash of Orange Bitters
One-half Italian Vermouth
One-half French Vermouth (Stir)

NEWMAN   Dash of Amer Picon Bitters
One-third French Vermouth
One-third Italian Vermouth
One-third Plymouth Gin

Patronymic of a man who for a time ran the old Haymarket, a widely famed Tenderloin resort.

NEW ORLEANS   Dash of Orange Bitters
One jigger Italian Vermouth
Shake; fizz glass; fill from siphon

NEWPORT   One-fifth Italian Vermouth
Two-fifths French Vermouth
Two-fifths Gordon Gin
Orange Peel

NORMANDIE   Dash of Orange Bitters

One-half jigger Apple Whiskey
One-half Italian Vermouth (Stir)

The name of a hotel in Broadway's early spotlight district, patronized by sportsmen and sports.

NUMBER THREE   One dash Orange Bitters
One dash Anisette
One-quarter French Vermouth
Three-quarters Nicholson Gin
Squeeze Lemon Peel on top

NUTTING   Dash of Orange Bitters
One-half French Vermouth
One-half Plymouth Gin (Stir)

Its namesake was Col. Andrew J. Nutting, of Brooklyn, an ardent patron of the Bar for many years.

OJEN   One teaspoon Peychaud Bitters
One jigger Ojen
Serve in claret glass with Seltzer

OLD-FASHIONED One-quarter lump Sugar
WHISKEY   Two spoons Water
One dash Angostura
One jigger Whiskey
One piece Lemon Peel
One lump Ice
Serve with small spoon

This was brought to the Old Waldorf in the days of its "sit-down" Bar, and was introduced by, or in honor of, Col. James E. Pepper, of Kentucky, proprietor of a celebrated whiskey of the period. It was said to have been the invention of a bartender at the famous Pendennis Club in Louisville, of which Col. Pepper was a member.

OLIVET

Dash of Orange Bitters
One-half Tom Gin
One-half Italian Vermouth
Stir; one Olive in glass

OPAL

Dash of Orange Bitters
One-half Plymouth Gin
One-half French Vermouth
Stir; one dash of Absinthe on top

ORANGE
BLOSSOM

One-third Orange Juice
One-third Tom Gin
One-third Italian Vermouth

May have been named by a youthful bartender with romantic spring notions, though the weight of evidence ascribes it to some young bridegroom or other who wanted something novel to use at his final stag party.

ORANGE
BLOSSOM No. 2

One-half Orange Juice
One-half Gin (bar glass)

PALMETTO

Dash of Orange Bitters
One-half St. Croix Rum
One-half Italian Vermouth (Stir)

PAN-AMERICAN

One-half Lemon, muddled
Three dashes Syrup
One jigger Whiskey

PASSIPE

One-third French Vermouth
Two-thirds House of Lords Gin
Juice of one Orange

PEACOCK | Two dashes Amer Picon Bitters
One dash Absinthe
One jigger Brandy

PEG O'
MY HEART | One-half Lime Juice
One-half Bacardi Rum
Color with Grenadine

PELL | One-half Italian Vermouth
One-half Nicholson Gin (Olive)

PEPLO | A Pousse Café, shaken and strained
(See "Fancy Potations and Otherwise")

PERFECT | One-third Italian Vermouth
One-third French Vermouth
One-third Plymouth Gin
Frappé with an Orange Peel

PERFECT No. 2 | One-third Gin
One-third Italian Vermouth
One-third French Vermouth (Stir)
Serve with a green Olive
Twist piece of Lemon Peel on top

PICK-ME-UP | Two dashes Acid or Lemon Phos-
phate
One-half Italian Vermouth
One-half Absinthe

PING PONG | Dash of Orange Bitters
One-half Sloe Gin
One-half French Vermouth

Named after a game said to have originated in England, but which was installed in the big room next to the Old Waldorf Bar in its early days. Bar habitués learned to play it, but sometimes experienced difficulty in hitting the right ball, claiming three or four were going over the net at one time, instead of one.

POET'S DREAM   One-third Benedictine
One-third French Vermouth
One-third dry Gin
Lemon Peel squeezed on top

POLO   One-fourth Lemon Juice
One-fourth Orange Juice
One-half Rum

Not after Marco, the adventurer, but after the game which, during the "Nineties," was little known except to the fashionable. That was before Meadowbrook had hurled its young men and its wealth into a comparative void in our National outdoor life.

POMEROY   One-third French Vermouth
One-third Italian Vermouth
One-third Gordon Gin
One Orange Peel

PORTO RICO   Sloe Gin Rickey with dash of
Grenadine

PRAIRIE   One pony Tom Gin
(Often called   One Egg, in claret glass
"Prairie Chicken")   A little Pepper and Salt
Cover with Gin
Serve with napkin

PRINCE

Two dashes Orange Bitters in glass
Whiskey
Two dashes Crème de Menthe on top

PRINCE HENRY *

Martini, with dash of Crème de Menthe

PRINCETON

Dash of Orange Bitters
Two-thirds jigger Tom Gin
Stir; fill with Seltzer

After a college somewhere in New Jersey, which used to send a lot of young men to the Old Waldorf Bar. Or, at least, they came.

QUEEN

One-third Italian Vermouth
One-third French Vermouth
One-third Gin
Frappé with fine slice of Pineapple

RACQUET CLUB *

Dash of Orange Bitters
One-half Plymouth Gin
One-half French Vermouth
Orange Peel

RALEIGH

Juice of one-half Lime
Juice of one-half Orange
Pony of Bacardi Rum
Dash of Grenadine Syrup

REES

Wash inside of mixing glass with green Absinthe

One dash Angostura Bitters
One-tenth Italian Vermouth
Nine-tenths Tom Gin (no Ice)

RIDING CLUB *   Dash of Angostura Bitters
One-half pony Acid Phosphate
One jigger Red Calisaya (Stir)

ROBERT BURNS   Dash of Orange Bitters
One dash of Absinthe
One-quarter Italian Vermouth
Three-quarters Scotch Whiskey
(Stir)

It may have been named after the celebrated Scots-
man. Chances are, however, that it was christened in
honor of a cigar salesman, who "bought" in the Old Bar.

ROBIN   One-half Calisaya Bitters
One-half Scotch Whiskey
Stir; serve with a Cherry

ROB ROY *   Dash of Orange Bitters
One-half Scotch
One-half Italian Vermouth
(Stir)

RORY O'MORE   Dash of Angostura Bitters
One-half Irish Whiskey
One-half Italian Vermouth
(Stir)

ROSE   One-fourth Grand Marnier
Three-quarters Dry Gin (Stir)

ROSEMARY *
  One-half French Vermouth
  One-half Bourbon Whiskey

ROSSINGTON
  One and one-half jiggers Italian
   Vermouth
  Two and one-half jiggers Gor-
   don Gin
  Peel of Orange on top

ROSSINGTON No. 2
  One-third Dry Gin
  One-third Italian Vermouth
  One-third French Vermouth
  Orange Peel

RUBY
  One-third French Vermouth
  Two-thirds Cherry Brandy
  Ten drops Acid Phosphate
  One dash Orange Bitters
  Two dashes Maraschino

RUSSIAN
  Two-thirds Brandy
  One-third Orange Juice
  Dash of Orange Bitters
  Dash of Absinthe

(Another "Russian" contained Vodka, but was seldom called for.)

ST. FRANCIS *
  Two dashes Gordon Orange
   Bitters
  One-half Gordon Gin
  One-half French Vermouth
  Serve with stuffed Olive

ST. JOHN *
  Martini, with dash of Orange
   Bitters and Lemon Peel
   (whiskey glass)

ST. PETER *

Juice of two Limes
One-fourth teaspoon Sugar
One-half jigger Gordon Gin

SALOMÉ *

Two dashes Absinthe
One-half Italian Vermouth
One-half Dubonnet (Stir)

SAM WARD

Cup a small Lemon
Fill with fine Ice
Fill with Yellow Chartreuse

SANTIAGO

One-half Orange Juice
One-half Bacardi Rum
Color with Grenadine

SAVANNAH

Juice one-half Orange
Drink of Gin
White of one Egg (claret glass)
Dash of Crème de Cacao

SAZERAC

Few dashes of Peychaud Bitters
Dash of Absinthe
Dash of Italian Vermouth
One jigger Bourbon or Scotch

SEPTEMBER
MORN *

Juice of one Lime
One jigger Bacardi Rum
White of one Egg (claret glass)
Color with Grenadine

SEPTEMBER
MORN No. 2

Clover Club; made with Bacardi instead of Gin

SHAFTER *

Dash of Orange Bitters

One-half Nicholson Gin
One-half Italian Vermouth (Stir)

SHAKE-UP-SILO One-half French Vermouth
One-half Plymouth Gin

SHERMAN Dash each, Angostura and Orange Bitters
Three dashes Absinthe
Two-thirds jigger Italian Vermouth
One third jigger Whiskey

SILVER Martini, with dash of Maraschino

SIR JASPER Dash of Orange Bitters
One-third Italian Vermouth
One-third French Vermouth
One-third Tom Gin (Stir)
Twist Lemon Peel on top

SLOE GIN Dash of Orange Bitters
Two-thirds Sloe Gin
One-third Plymouth Gin (Stir)

SODA Two dashes Angostura Bitters
Two lumps Ice (Collins glass)
Two pieces Lemon Peel
One bottle Lemon Soda

SOMERSET One-fourth Italian Vermouth
One-fourth French Vermouth
One-half Tom Gin (Stir)

SOUL KISS One-third French Vermouth
Two-thirds Dry Gin

White of Egg (bar glass)

After a musical comedy of that name, which, because of its appellation, stirred up a good many ideas among the young—and middle-aged—about the latter part of the first decade of the century.

SOUTHGATE	One-fourth lump Sugar dissolved in one-half pony of Water Dash of Boonekamp Bitters One jigger Whiskey One piece twisted Lemon Peel
STAR	Dash of Orange Bitters One-half Apple Whiskey One-half Italian Vermouth (Stir)
STEPHEN'S	One-third Sherry One-third French Vermouth One-third Benedictine
STRAWBERRY	Dash of Orange Bitters Juice of twelve Strawberries, or one pony of Syrup Three-quarters Brandy One dash of Maraschino (Stir) Strawberry in glass
SUBURBAN *	Dash of Orange Bitters Dash of Angostura Bitters One-fifth Port Wine One-fifth Jamaica Rum Three-fifths Whiskey
SUNSHINE	Dash of Orange Bitters One-eighth Italian Vermouth

One-eighth French Vermouth
Three-fourths Tom Gin

SWAN

Juice of one Lime
One-half jigger Swan Gin
One-half jigger French Vermouth
Two dashes Angostura Bitters
Two dashes Absinthe

TANGO

One-half French Vermouth
One-half Dry Gin
White of Egg

After the Argentinian dance which first became popular during the early days of the modern dance craze, in 1912 or 1913.

TANGO No. 2

One-fifth French Vermouth
One-fifth Italian Vermouth
One-fifth Rum
One-fifth Benedictine
One-fifth Orange Juice

THANKSGIVING

No Bitters
One-half Italian Vermouth
One-half Tom Gin
Piece of Orange Peel

THIRD DEGREE *

One-eighth French Vermouth
Seven-eighths Plymouth Gin
Several dashes Absinthe

THOMPSON

One-third Italian Vermouth
Two-thirds Whiskey
One piece each of Orange Peel,
    Pineapple, Lemon Peel

After Denman Thompson, the actor, who made "The Old Homestead" famous, and upon whom that play had equally beneficent results.

THREE-TO-ONE   One-half Lime Juice
One-third Apricot Brandy
Two-thirds Dry Gin

TIPPERARY   Two-thirds Sloe Gin
One-third French Vermouth
Teaspoon of Lemon Juice
Invented long before the wartime song of that name was heard, so that it must be considered a direct namesake of an Irish county, and so called by a fond exile.

TIP TOP   Four dashes Benedictine
Two dashes Angostura Bitters
One jigger French Vermouth (Stir)
Serve with Lemon Peel

TOM GIN   Dash of Orange Bitters
One jigger Tom Gin (Stir)

TRILBY *   Dash of Orange Bitters
One-third French Vermouth
Two-thirds Tom Gin
One dash of Crème Yvette (Stir)

TURF   Dash of Angostura Bitters
One-third Italian Vermouth
Two-thirds Holland Gin (Stir)
At times a good half—possibly two-thirds—of the crowd in the Bar were interested in racing.

TUXEDO   Dash of Orange Bitters
                    Two-thirds Plymouth Gin
                    One-third Sherry (Stir)
After a settlement on the Erie R. R. where many
customers of the Bar had country places.

TYRONE   Dash of Orange Bitters
                    Two-thirds Sloe Gin
                    One-third Italian Vermouth (Stir)

UNION   Dash of Orange Bitters
LEAGUE *   One-third Port Wine
                    Two-thirds Tom Gin (Stir)

VANDERVERE   One-half Nicholson Gin
                    One-quarter French Vermouth
                    One-quarter Italian Vermouth (Stir)
                    Twist Lemon Peel on top

VAN WYCK   Dash of Orange Bitters
                    One-third Sloe Gin
                    Two-thirds Tom Gin

VERMOUTH   Dash of Orange Bitters
(French)   One jigger French Vermouth

VERMOUTH   Dash of Orange Bitters
(Italian)   One jigger Italian Vermouth

VIN MARIANI   Dash of Orange Bitters
                    One-third Italian Vermouth
                    Two-thirds Vin Mariani

VIVARY   Dash of Orange Bitters
                    One-half Italian Vermouth

One-half French Vermouth
One dash Absinthe

WALDORF
Dash of Manhattan Bitters
One-third Whiskey
One-third Absinthe
One-third Italian Vermouth

WALDORF-
ASTORIA
Pony of Benedictine on Ice
Cover and build mound with sweet-
ened Whipped Cream

WALDORF
GLOOM-LIFTER
Juice one-half Lemon
One-half teaspoon Brandy
One jigger Irish Whiskey
White of one Egg
One-half teaspoon Sugar
Dash of Raspberry Syrup
Dash of Grenadine

WALL STREET
One-third Italian Vermouth
Two-thirds Gordon Gin
Squeeze of Orange Peel on top

WALTER
MONTEITH
One-half Italian Vermouth
One-half Nicholson Gin

WEST INDIA
Dash of Angostura Bitters
One-half Tom Gin
One-half French Vermouth (Stir)

WHISKEY
Dash of Angostura Bitters
One dash Gin
One jigger of Whiskey (Stir)
See also Old-Fashioned Whiskey.

WHITE
ELEPHANT

One-third Italian Vermouth
Two-thirds Dry Gin
White of one Egg

WHITE
GRAPE-JUICE

Fill lemonade glass two-thirds with
   Ice and Grape Juice
Add Juice of Lime
Fill with Seltzer

H. P. WHITNEY

One-quarter Italian Vermouth
One-quarter French Vermouth
One-half Plymouth Gin
Frappé with Orange Peel

A noted patron of the turf who frequented the Bar
before he and his friends moved up to the Brook Club.

WHITTAKER

Dash of Orange Bitters
One-third Italian Vermouth
Two-thirds Red Calisaya (Stir)

WIDOW

One-half jigger Gordon Gin
One-half jigger French Vermouth
Juice of an Orange

WILD CHERRY

Dash of Orange Bitters
One-half Tom Gin
One-half Cherry Brandy (Stir)

WOXUM

One-half pony Yellow Chartreuse
One-half jigger Apple Whiskey
One-half jigger Italian Vermouth
   (Stir)

Some think it is aboriginally American, and ascribe

it to a "bunch of Indians," so-called, who occasionally made whoopee—or, as it was said at that time, "raised hell"—in the Old Waldorf Bar when they could get away with it.

YALE   Dash of Orange Bitters
         One-half Tom Gin
         One-half Italian Vermouth (Stir)
         Little Seltzer on top

An institution somewhere beyond Old Greenwich, where many young men go for the purpose of commuting to New York for week-ends. The Old Bar used to be one of their "ports of call" and there they used to find many who in years past had gone to the same place and done the same things.

YORK   Dash of Orange Bitters
         One-half French Vermouth
         One-half Scotch Whiskey (Stir)

ZAZA *   One dash Orange Bitters
         One-half Plymouth Gin
         One-half Calisaya (Stir)

ZAZA No. 2   Two dashes Orange Bitters
         One-third Tom Gin
         Two-thirds Dubonnet (Stir)

1915   One-third Curaçao
         One-third Cream
         One-third Gin

Named in honor of a New Year. Some believe this was the last cocktail invented in the Old Waldorf Bar.

FANCY POTATIONS AND OTHERWISE *

Note: The type of serving-glass appears in parenthesis at the end of one line of most formulas.

COBBLERS

COBBLER: A summer drink made of iced wine, sugar, fruit juices, etc. [U.S.]

CLARET
One spoon Sugar
Two ponies of Water
One and one-half jiggers Claret
Fill with Ice; fruit well (goblet)

NARRAGANSETT
Whole peel of Orange
Juice of one Orange
One jigger Whiskey
One bottle Ginger Ale
Stir (Collins glass)

SHERRY
One-fourth spoon Sugar
One pony of Water
One and one-half jigger Sherry
Stir; fill with Ice; fruit (goblet)

COOLERS

COOLER: A refreshing beverage—supposed to illustrate its name.

BOSTON
Juice one-half Lemon
One-quarter spoon Sugar

* In "Drinks from Other Climes" will be found numerous other classified and miscellaneous mixed drinks.

                One jigger Medford Rum
                Ice; one bottle plain Soda (Collins glass)

HAWAII   Whole peel of Orange
                Juice of one Orange
                One jigger Whiskey
                Ice; fill Collins glass with Ginger Ale

HILLY CROFT   Whole rind of Lemon
                Two lumps Ice
                One Ginger Ale
                One jigger Tom Gin

KLONDIKE   Whole peel of one Orange
                Juice of Orange
                One jigger Whiskey
                Ice; one Ginger Ale (Collins glass)

REMSEN   Whole peel of Lemon
                One jigger Tom Gin
                Ice; fill with plain Soda

ROOFGARDEN   One dash Bitters, on one lump Sugar
                One jigger French Vermouth
                Ice; one bottle of Ginger Ale (Collins)

SEAWANHAKA
YACHT CLUB   Whole peel of one Lemon
                Two lumps Ice
                One jigger Whiskey
                Fill with Ginger Ale (goblet)

CUPS

CUP: A beverage made with wine, generally iced, and with flavoring herbs and fruits. In olden times, vegetables were also included, particularly cucumbers.

CHAMPAGNE
(pitcher)

One and one-half ponies Brandy
One pony Benedictine
One pony Maraschino
One bottle Soda
One bottle Wine
One stick Ice
Fruit; decorate with Mint

CLARET CUP
WALDORF
(pitcher)

One-half spoon Sugar
One and one-half ponies Brandy
Pony each, Benedictine and Maraschino
Seltzer to fill glass
Stir; pour into pitcher; large stick Ice
One bottle Claret
Fruit; decorate with frosted Mint

FRUIT
(pitcher)

Equal portions, Raspberry Syrup, Strawberry Syrup, Pineapple Syrup
Lemon and Orange Juice
Currant Syrup
Add Seltzer or Apollinaris to fill
Add sliced Bananas and Strawberries

HOBSON'S KISS

Champagne, Moselle, or Rhine Wine Cup
Made like Claret Cup Waldorf
Commemorating a notable osculation by which enthu-

siastic women, upon his return from Cuban waters, came
near dimming the fame of Lieut. Commander Richard
Pearson Hobson, U.S.N., who had sunk the collier
Merrimac in a heroic effort to bottle up the Spanish
fleet in Santiago harbor, during the Spanish-American
War.

MINEHEART   Equal portions, Raspberry Syrup, Pine-
                    apple Juice, Lemon Juice, Orange
                    Juice, Red Currant Juice
              Stir; add Ice; fill with Water
                    Add sliced bananas and whole straw-
                    berries

FIZZES

Fizz: An effervescing beverage, named, onomatopoetically, from
the noise.

BALTIMORE   One-half pony Anisette
BRACER   One-half pony Brandy
              White of one Egg (fizz glass)
              Frappé; fizz with Carbonic

BAYARD   One dash Raspberry
BEAUTY   One dash Maraschino
              One spoon Lemon Juice
              One jigger Tom Gin (lemonade)
              Ice; shake; strain; fill with Seltzer

BISMARCK   Juice one-half Lemon
              One-half spoon Sugar
              One pony Raspberry Syrup
              One and one-half jigger Rhine Wine

Shake and strain; fill with chilled
Seltzer

CHICAGO   Juice one-fourth Lemon
One-half spoon Sugar
White of one Egg
One-half jigger Jamaica Rum
One-half jigger Port Wine
Ice; shake; strain; fill from siphon

An importation from the Windy City long before
bombs, machine guns and sawed-off shotguns had come
to disturb its peaceful life.

FREE SILVER   Juice one-fourth Lemon
One-third spoon Sugar
Two-thirds Tom Gin
One-third Medford Rum
One-half pony of Milk
Ice; shake; strain; fill from siphon

Free silver was an obsession of a great many Americans during the final decade of the last century.

GIN   Juice one-half Lemon
One-half spoon Sugar
One jigger Tom Gin
Shake and strain; fill from chilled
siphon

GOLDEN   Juice one-half Lemon
One-half spoon Sugar
Yolk one Egg
One jigger Gin
Shake; strain; fill from chilled siphon

GRENADINE

Juice one-half Lemon
One-half spoon Sugar
One pony Grenadine
One pony Milk
One jigger Tom Gin
Ice; shake; strain; fill from siphon

HORTON

Gin fizz, with three or four sprigs
of Mint, shaken up

JAP

Juice one-half Lemon
One spoonful Sugar
One-half jigger each of Rye Whiskey
and Port Wine
White of one Egg
Frappé; strain; serve with Seltzer
and one slice Pineapple

MORNING
GLORY

Juice one-half Lemon
One-half spoon Sugar
White of one Egg
One jigger Scotch
Two dashes Absinthe
Shake; strain; fill from chilled
siphon

MURDOCK

Two lumps Ice, dissolved in pony
of Water
Two pieces Lemon Peel
One jigger Rye Whiskey
Fill glass with Ice
Fizz from siphon

NEW ORLEANS   Juice of one Lemon and a half
White of Egg
One spoon Sugar
Three dashes Orange Water
One jigger Cream
One jigger Gin
Ice; shake well (goblet)

ROYAL   Gin Fizz with a whole Egg (lemonade)
Fill from chilled siphon

SILVER   Gin Fizz, with White of Egg
Fill with Seltzer

STRAWBERRY   One pony Strawberry Syrup
Juice of one-half Lemon
One jigger Tom Gin (lemonade)
Ice; shake; strain; fill from siphon

WHISKEY   Juice of one-half Lemon
One spoon Sugar
One jigger Whiskey
Ice; shake; strain; fill from siphon

WHISKEY
No. 2   One-half spoon Sugar
One-half pony of Water
Three or four lumps Ice
One jigger Whiskey
Three slices of Fruit
Serve with spoon

FLIPS

FLIP: A drink made with some liquor, mixed with an egg and spiced and sugared.

SHERRY
    One Egg (star glass)
    One-half spoon Sugar
    One jigger Sherry
    Ice; shake; strain; grate Nutmeg on top

Note: Other flips made by the same formula, with other bases than Sherry.

KRUGER
SPECIAL
    Sherry Flip, with a dash of Grenadine
       (fizz glass)
    Fill from siphon

WHISKEY
    One Egg
    One-half spoon Sugar
    One jigger Whiskey
    Shake; strain; Nutmeg grated on top

HIGH-BALLS

Just as is the case with "cocktail," the origin and application of "high-ball" as a name for a stimulant is open to discussion. Some have asserted that the name was taken from the National Game, possibly because of the effect upon the "batting average" of one who "hits" enough in rapid succession. However the lexicographer digs further.

In slang, a drink is often described as a "shot"; in Pall-Mall English it's a "spot." High-ball, more or less pure American for what a Britisher calls a Whiskey-and-Soda, say the learned, is combined from "high," meaning tall, and descriptive of the container, and "ball," which used to be the equivalent of "shot," both metallically and absorbatively. Therefore the classical definition, "a 'long' drink consisting of whiskey, to which is added soda-water, mineral water or some other effervescent, served in a tall glass with broken ice."

HIGH-BALL   One jigger Whiskey
                  One lump Ice
                  Fill from siphon

The whiskey might be Scotch, Bourbon, Rye or Irish; or instead might be used Gin, Sloe Gin, Brandy or Rum, the particular High-ball taking its name from the liquor used. In a GINGER ALE HIGH-BALL, Ginger Ale is used instead of aerated water.

BERMUDA   One-third Brandy
                  One-third Plymouth Gin
                  One-third French Vermouth
                  One whole Lemon Peel
                  One lump Ice; fill from siphon

PALL MALL   One-third Nicholson Gin
                  One-third Vermouth
                  One-third Brandy
                  Fill from chilled siphon

HOT POTATIONS

COLUMBIA   One-half lump Sugar
SKILL   Two spoons hot Water
                  One piece twisted Lemon Peel
                  One jigger Whiskey
                  Fill with hot Water; small spoon

Called after the prowess Columbia had exhibited in a certain boat race with Cornell, and first composed upon the demand of a Columbia "fan" for a new drink that would properly commemorate the occasion.

HOT GIN SLING See the same under "SLINGS"

HOT SCOTCH	Lump Sugar, dissolved in hot Water One jigger Scotch Fill two-thirds with hot Water One piece Lemon Peel, twisted
HOT SHERRY	Half lump Sugar, dissolved in hot Water One jigger Sherry Fill two-thirds with hot Water Nutmeg on side
HOT SPICED RUM	Lump Sugar, dissolved in hot Water One jigger Rum Five whole Cloves Fill glass with hot Water
HOT WHISKEY SKIN	Lump Sugar, dissolved in hot Water One jigger Whiskey One piece twisted Lemon Peel Fill with hot Water
LOCOMOTIVE HOT (pitcher)	Yolks of three Eggs, well beaten One ounce of Honey Five Cloves One pony of Triple Sec One pint Hot Burgundy Stir well; serve in hot glasses
MULLED CLARET or Burgundy	Three spoons Sugar One-half pint Water Five or six Cloves Three small pieces Cinnamon Whole rind of Lemon, cut very thin

Let come to a boil; add Wine
Boil again and serve very hot

TOM AND
JERRY

Beat six Eggs well, adding Powdered Sugar until very thick, working out all lumps
Pour one-half tablespoon of this batter into mug
One-half jigger Brandy
One-half jigger Jamaica Rum
Fill with hot Water; add Nutmeg
(See also TODDIES, and "Drinks from Other Climes")

HOT—WITH FLAMES

BLUE BLAZES

One lump Sugar dissolved in one-half jigger hot Water (ale mug)
One jigger Scotch
Set fire to Whiskey; pour back and forth blazing

CAFÉ BRÛLER

Moisten edge of claret glass—dip in Powdered Sugar
Seven-eighths Hot Coffee
One-eighth Brandy on top
Set fire to Brandy

JERSEY
FLASHLIGHT

Two lumps Sugar
One dash Angostura Bitters
One piece Lemon Peel
One jigger Apple Whiskey
Fill with hot Water; ignite the whole
Mix while blazing

JULEPS

JULEP: From the Spanish *julepe*, itself derived from the Arabic and Persian *julab* = *gul* (rose) plus *ab* (water); so that the name is of ancient origin. Today, fresh Mint, as part of a julep, is as unchanging as an old-time Persian law.

BRANDY

Put three or four sprigs of Mint in mixing glass
One-half spoon Sugar
One pony Brandy
One pony Water; crush well
Fill goblet two-thirds with Ice
Strain mixture on top
Fruit well; decorate with Mint

CHAMPAGNE

One lump Sugar
Three sprigs Mint
Two lumps Ice
Fill with Champagne

MINT

In mixer put three sprigs Mint
One-half spoon Sugar
One pony Water
Press well, crushing Mint
Add one jigger Whiskey; stir
Pour into glass two-thirds full Ice
Fruit well; decorate with Mint

PRESBREY

Three sprigs Mint
One jigger Whiskey
One dash St. Croix Rum; shaved Ice; stir; Fruit and Mint

WHISKEY MINT

Three sprigs Mint
One-half spoon Sugar

One pony of Water
Press well and add jigger Whiskey
Ice; stir; strain well

POUSSE CAFÉS

L'AMOUR

One-third Maraschino
Yolk of one Egg
Cover with Vanilla
Fill with Brandy

RAINBOW

Equal parts of Grenadine, Mara-
schino, Green Crème de Menthe,
Yellow Chartreuse, Curaçao and
Brandy

WALDORF

One seventh each, Raspberry Syrup,
Anisette, Parfait d'Amour,
Crème Yvette, Yellow Char-
treuse, Green Chartreuse and
Brandy (Sherry glass)

PUNCHES

Contrary to common belief, the punch is not exactly an English invention. In its original form the word was the Sanskrit *pancha*, meaning "five." The Hindus used five ingredients to make what they called *panch*—Arrack, tea, sugar, water and lemon. Some attribute its importation into England, not to early British travelers in the Orient, but to the British East India Company, in its efforts to popularize tea. If that looks a bit far-fetched, in modern punches the rule of five ingredients does not always apply.

In addition to the various punches served at the Old Waldorf-Astoria, several scores of others are made in various parts of the world. He or she who complains of lack of "punch" among the drinks listed in this book is advised to consult a standard book of punch recipes.

BOSTON MILK Grate Nutmeg in glass
One-half spoon Sugar
One-half jigger Whiskey
One-half St. Croix Rum (goblet)
Fill with chilled Milk; shake well;
strain

BRANDY Juice of one-half Lemon
One-half spoon Sugar
One pony of Water
One jigger Brandy
Ice; shake; strain; fruit

CHAMPAGNE One pint Champagne
(pitcher) One pint white Beaune, or other white
Wine
One pint Apollinaris
One sliced Orange
Two lumps Sugar; Ice

CHAMPAGNE One pint Champagne
(KINSLEY) One pint Burgundy
One pint Apollinaris
Three lumps Sugar
One sliced Orange; Ice

CLARET Juice one-half Lemon
One-half spoon Sugar
One pony of Water
One and one-half jiggers Claret
Ice; stir; pour into goblet; fruit well

CLARET No. 2 (gallon)	Juice six Lemons Two ponies each, Curaçao and Brandy Tablespoon Sugar Two quarts Claret Ice; two siphons of Seltzer
CREAM	One-half spoon Sugar One pony White Curaçao One pony Brandy Fill two-thirds with chilled Milk Shake well; strain; Nutmeg
CUBAN MILK	One pony Vanilla One-half teaspoon Sugar One whole Egg One pony Bacardi Fill with Milk; shake; strain; Nutmeg
FISH-HOUSE	Juice one-half Lemon One-half spoon Sugar One-half jigger Brandy One-half jigger Jamaica Rum Ice; shake well; fruit in season
GOODWIN	Juice one Lime Open spoon Sugar One dash Sherry One jigger Rye Ice; shake; strain; fruit
HERALD	Juice of one Orange One-half spoon Sugar

One jigger Whiskey
Ice; shake; fruit; flavor with St.
Croix Rum

KNICKERBOCKER   Juice one-half Lemon
One-half spoon Sugar
One pony Water
One jigger St. Croix Rum
Ice; stir; fruit well; float Claret
on top

LANDER'S   One-fourth Jamaica Rum
One-fourth Gordon Gin
One-fourth French Vermouth
One-fourth Lemon Juice; Frappé

MILK   One jigger Whiskey (or Brandy)
One-half spoon Sugar
Fill three-quarters with Milk
Ice; shake; strain; serve with
Nutmeg

PEGGY O'NEILL   One dash Parfait d'Amour
One Lime Peel in center of glass
One drink Rye Whiskey
Three sprigs Mint
Ice; fill with Seltzer

After an opera or play of that name, it is believed.
The original Peggy O'Neill was the daughter of a Washington tavern-keeper, and noted for her beauty and
wit.

PING PONG   Juice of one Lemon
One dash Bitters

One jigger Apple Cider
Fresh Egg
One spoon Sugar
Shake; strain; fill with chilled Soda

PING PONG
No. 2
(pitcher)

Five siphons
One quart Whiskey
One quart Brandy
Crushed Mint; Fruit

PLANTER'S

Juice of one small Lime
Jigger of Jamaica Rum
Fruit like a Claret Punch
Fill glass from chilled siphon

PUNCH
UNIVERSAL

Two tablespoons Sugar
Juice of two Lemons and one
    Orange
One pony Jamaica Rum
One pony Brandy
One bottle plain Soda
One quart Chablis; Ice; Fruit

ROMAN

Juice of one-half Lemon
One spoon Sugar
One pony Curaçao
One-half jigger Jamaica Rum
One-half Brandy
One or two dashes Port Wine
Ice; shake; strain; Seltzer on top;
    Fruit

ROOSEVELT

Muddle one-half Lemon
One spoon Sugar

One jigger Apple Whiskey
Ice; shake; one dash of Brandy on
    top

RUM

Juice of one-half Lemon
One-half spoon Sugar
One pony of Water
One jigger Rum
Fill glass two-thirds fine Ice; Fruit

SCHLEY

Juice and rind of one-half Lime
One-fourth spoon Sugar
One-third jigger St. Croix Rum
Two-thirds jigger Whiskey
Ice; shake; strain; fill with Seltzer

SHERIDAN

Plain lemonade, with Whiskey
    on top

STEINWAY

Muddle one-half Lemon
One-half spoon Sugar
One jigger Whiskey
Fill with chilled Seltzer
Stir; strain; Fruit

Named after Charles Steinway, a well-known gourmet.

WALDORF

Whiskey, with Claret floated on top

WHISKEY

Juice of one-half Lemon
One-half spoon Sugar
One pony of Water
Fill glass two-thirds with fine Ice
One jigger Whiskey
Stir; fruit well in season

WHISKEY MILK   One-half spoon Sugar
One jigger Whiskey
Fill three-quarters with chilled Milk
Shake well; strain; Nutmeg on top

RICKEYS

The Rickey owes its name to Colonel "Joe" Rickey, though an interested public has long persisted in referring to him as "Colonel Jim" Rickey. Colonel Rickey had been a lobbyist in Washington, and as such used to buy drinks for members of Congress in the glamorous days before they had come to depend upon the discreet activities of gentlemen in green hats to keep them wet while they voted dry. The drink was invented and named for him at Shoemaker's, famous in Washington as a Congressional hangout.

GIN RICKEY   Juice and rind of one Lime
Lump of Ice (goblet)
Gin to suit customer
Fill from siphon
Note: Other Rickeys get their names from the liquor taking the place of Gin in following the formula.

SANGAREES

The Sangaree probably acquired its name for one or two reasons, or both. The word is derived from the Spanish *sanguia*, meaning "bloody," which itself comes from the Latin *sanguis* (blood), and a sangaree is red, or reddish—or was as originally made. The other reason for the name may be that it is supposed to have a cooling effect upon the blood.

SANGAREE   One-half jigger French Vermouth
One-half jigger Sloe Gin
One dash Acid Phosphate

Two dashes Angostura Bitters
Fill with Ice (fizz glass)

PORT WINE   One-half spoon Sugar
One jigger Water
One and one-half jiggers Port Wine
Ice; stir; strain

Other Sangarees were made similarly of Sherry, or
Gin, or Brandy. (See "Drinks from Other Climes.")

SLINGS

SLING: Name, but not the drink itself, ascribed to the German
schlingen, meaning "swallow," not from the English verb meaning to
"hurl"—down.

BRANDY   One-half lump Sugar dissolved in two
spoons Water (whiskey glass)
One jigger Brandy
One piece twisted Lemon Peel
One lump Ice; serve with small spoon

GIN   One lump Sugar, dissolved in half
wine-glass Water
One-half glass Gin
One lump Ice
Stir with spoon; grated Nutmeg

HOT GIN   One lump Sugar, dissolved in hot
Water
One jigger Gin; more hot Water
One piece Lemon Peel

WHISKEY   Half lump Sugar in half pony Water
One jigger Whiskey

Four or five drops Lemon Juice
One piece Lemon Peel; Ice (spoon)

SMASHES

SMASH: To flatten; in tennis, to bat, etc.; in slang a smash is something of extraordinary ability. Somewhere in these lies the origin of the term as "a beverage of spirituous liquors, with mint, water, sugar and ice."

BRANDY

Two sprigs Mint
Two spoons Water,
One-quarter spoon Sugar
Muddle in fizz glass
One jigger Brandy
Two lumps Ice; serve with small spoon

WHISKEY

Three sprigs of Mint
Fill mixing glass with fine Ice
Two more sprigs of Mint
One-quarter spoon Sugar
One-half pony of Water
Press well; add one jigger Whiskey
Stir; strain; fruit well; Mint on top

SOURS

SOUR: A good old Anglo-Saxon word, and it started as *surigan*, was shortened to *sur*, and finally in its more modern version became the name of an alcoholic drink because of the taste of the lemon or lime that is an essential.

BRANDY

Juice one-half Lemon (star glass)
One-half spoon Sugar

One jigger Brandy
Fill with Ice; stir; strain; fruit

BRUNSWICK

Juice one-half Lemon
One spoon Sugar
One jigger Rye
Ice, Stir; fruit; Claret on top

Invented at the Old Hotel Brunswick, once a resort for Fashion, and situated on the north side of Madison Square.

DOUBLE
STANDARD

Juice one-half Lime
One-half Rye Whiskey
One-half Tom Gin
One dash Raspberry Syrup
Ice; stir; strain; fruit

Owes its name to a controversy which during the Nineties divided two political parties on the subject of whether this country should have both a gold and silver standard of currency, or gold alone. Nothing to do with masculine or feminine conduct.

HANCOCK

Four dashes Rock Candy Syrup
Juice one Lime
Three dashes Jamaica Rum
One jigger Bourbon
Ice; stir; strain; Carbonic (fizz glass)

PEQUOD SOUR

Juice of one-half Lemon
One-half spoon Sugar
Two sprigs Mint
One-half Water

> One jigger Whiskey
> Stir well; fruit

ROOSEVELT   Juice of one-half Lemon
One-half spoon Sugar
One jigger Apple Whiskey
Ice; shake; strain on Fruit in glass

    Nothing to do with the New Deal; named to compliment the author of the Square Ditto.

RUM   Juice of one-half Lemon
One-half spoon Sugar
One jigger Rum
Ice; shake; strain on Fruit in glass

ST. CROIX   Juice of one-half Lemon
One spoon Sugar
One jigger St. Croix Rum
Ice; shake; strain on Fruit in glass

SANTIAGO   Juice of one-half Lemon
One-half spoon Sugar
One pony of Water
One jigger Whiskey
Ice; stir well; stuffed Olive in glass

SOUTHERN   St. Croix Sour, with Claret on top

WHISKEY   Juice of one-half Lemon
One-half spoon Sugar
One-half pony of Water
One jigger Whiskey
Ice; stir well; strain; fruit

TODDIES

Toddy: A general name for alcoholic liquor. Specifically and as herein applied, a beverage made of spirits, sugar and water, the latter usually hot, and sometimes with other ingredients for flavoring.

APPLE TODDY
COLD

Dissolve one lump of Sugar in three teaspoonfuls of Water (whiskey glass)
One jigger Apple Whiskey
One lump Ice
Serve with spoon and Nutmeg

(For Hot Apple Toddy, use larger glass and fill with hot water. Do not heat the Whiskey before mixing, and leave out the ice.)

BRANDY

One-half lump Sugar
Three spoons Water
One jigger Brandy
One lump Ice (whiskey glass)
Small spoon

BRANDY (Hot)

One teaspoon Sugar, dissolved in boiling Water
One wine-glass Brandy
Fill two-thirds with boiling Water
Grate Nutmeg on top

HOT BAKED
APPLE

One lump Sugar, dissolved
One-fourth Baked Apple
One jigger Apple Whiskey
Fill two-thirds with hot Water

HOT WHISKEY

One lump Sugar, dissolved in hot Water

One jigger Whiskey
Fill two-thirds with hot Water

KENTUCKY One-half lump Sugar
Two spoonfuls Water
One jigger Kentucky Whiskey

PEPSIN One-half lump Sugar
Two dashes Pepsin Bitters
One jigger Whiskey
One lump Ice
Fill from siphon

OTHER MIXED POTATIONS

ABSINTHE One jigger Absinthe (star)
FRAPPÉ Ice; shake well; strain
Fill with plain Water

ABSINTHE One jigger Absinthe
FRAPPÉ Ice; shake well; strain
(California) Fill from siphon

ANGEL'S BLUSH Two-thirds Benedictine (pony)
or KISS One-third Cream

ANGEL'S One-third Maraschino (pony)
DREAM One-third Cream
One-third Crème Yvette

ANGEL'S TIT Two-thirds Maraschino (pony)
One-third Cream

APRICOT   Cup one small Lemon
SAM WARD   Put in cocktail glass
                     Fill with fine Ice
                     Fill with Apricot Brandy

AUTOMOBILE   Juice one-half Lemon or Lime
                     One jigger Gordon Gin
                     Two lumps Ice (Collins glass)
                     Three sprigs Mint
                     One bottle Ginger Ale

First concocted in the days when the automobile was a novelty. The fact that its alcoholic content was modest, inclines one to the belief that it was not invented by the victim of a motor car.

BABY TITTY   One-third Anisette (sherry glass)
                     One-third Crème Yvette
                     One-third Whipped Cream
                     Serve with Cherry on top

BISHOP   Two jiggers Water
(pitcher)   Four spoons Sugar
                     Juice one-half Lemon
                     One jigger Jamaica Rum
                     One bottle Claret
                     Ice; fruit well

BORDELAISE   One pony Kirsch (lemonade glass)
                     One-half pony Raspberry Syrup
                     Ice; shake; strain; fill from siphon

BRADLEY   Pony of Crème de Menthe on Ice or
MARTIN   plain with Crème de Cacao on top

After the husband of a famous society leader who

gave a much publicized ball in the room adjoining the Old Waldorf Bar, while the latter was still building.

BRANDY AND GINGER ALE FRAPPÉ	One jigger Brandy (Collins glass) Fill with fine Ice Shake well; strain; fill with cold Ginger Ale
BRANDY CHAMPERELLE	One-third Curaçao (pony) One-third Boker's Bitters One-third Brandy
BRANDY FLOAT	Fill whiskey glass two-thirds with Seltzer Float pony of Brandy on top by using spoon
BRANDY SCAFFA	One-half Maraschino (pony) One-half Brandy Two dashes Angostura on top
CAFÉ KIRSCH	White of one Egg (claret glass) One-fourth spoon Sugar One pony each, Brandy, Kirschwasser and Coffee Ice, if preferred cold Shake well; strain
CASCADE	One pony Crème de Cassis (goblet) One pony French Vermouth Fizz with Seltzer
CHOCOLATE CREAM PHOSPHATE	Yolk one Egg (Collins glass) One pony Kirsch One pony Cream

Three dashes Acid Phosphate
Shake well; strain; fill with plain
　　Soda

CIDER NECTAR　Juice one-half Lemon
(one quart)　One spoon Sugar
　　Jigger each Brandy and Sherry
　　Ice; one quart Cider; Mint on top

CONCLAVE　Juice one Orange (goblet)
　　One pony Raspberry Syrup
　　Fill with chilled Milk; little Sugar;
　　　shake; strain

CREAM PUFF　One-half spoon Sugar (lemonade
　　　glass)
　　One pony Cream
　　One jigger St. Croix Rum
　　Ice; shake well; strain; fill from
　　　siphon

CREOLE LADY　Two Maraschino Cherries
　　One pony Maraschino
　　One sherry glass of Bourbon
　　One sherry glass of Old Madeira
　　Mix thoroughly with spoon—no Ice

DELGARCIA　Fill glass with Brandy (pony)
　　One slice Lemon laid flat on top
　　One lump Sugar on top of that—
　　　no Ice

DURKEE　One whole Lemon (Collins glass)
　　One spoon Sugar, muddled well

One jigger Jamaica Rum
Ice; fill with Soda; stir

EGG-NOG   One-half spoon Sugar (goblet)
One Egg
Fill three-quarters with Milk
Add Rum, Brandy, or Whiskey
Shake well; Nutmeg on top

FASCINATION   One-third White Curaçao
Two-thirds White Absinthe
One piece of Ice in champagne glass
Fill from siphon

FIN DE SIÈCLE   Tom Collins, with Grenadine and
Raspberry Syrup
Name dates it back to 1899 or 1900, when the term
was much used, but much mispronounced.

FLAMBEAU   Cup small Orange—turn inside out
One lump Sugar
One jigger Brandy (champagne
glass)
Set fire—burn five or ten seconds

FLORADORA   Juice one Lime (Collins glass)
One-half teaspoon Sugar
One-half pony Raspberry Syrup
One jigger Gin
Frappé; fizz with bottle Ginger Ale
After an English musical comedy that had a long run
at the Casino early in the century, and was famous for
its sextette, and for the number of wealthy marriages
made by the members of the latter.

GARDEN   One-half pony Crème Yvette
OF EDEN   One-half pony Apricot Brandy

GENERAL   One-half Lemon, muddled with
HENDRICKS   Two lumps Sugar in goblet
                One jigger Bourbon Whiskey
                Fill with chilled Apollinaris

GIN BUCK   One drink of Gin
                One Lemon in Collins glass; Ice
                One bottle imported Ginger Ale

GOLDEN   One-fourth yellow Chartreuse
SLIPPER   One small Egg (sherry glass)
                Fill with Eau de Vie de Dantzig

HAPPY   Equal parts, in claret glass of cracked
THOUGHT   Ice, of following:
                Anisette, Crème de Cacao,
                Crème de Rose, Crème de Menthe,
                Crème Yvette and Cognac

JIM RENWICK   Rind of one Lemon
                One jigger Whiskey
                Two lumps Ice (Collins glass)
                One bottle imported Ginger Ale

JOHN COLLINS   Juice one-half Lemon (Collins glass)
                One-half spoon Sugar
                One jigger Holland Gin
                Ice; shake; strain; fill with plain
                Soda
         One of two members of the Collins family famous

in bars in the old days. The difference between the two was that a Tom Collins was made with Old Tom Gin— or supposedly—while a John Collins was made with Holland Gin.

JOHN FRAZER	Seven-eighths pony Maraschino One-eighth Angostura Bitters
JOKER	One-fourth sherry glass each, Anisette, Crème Yvette, Benedictine and Cream
JONES LA POUSSE	Two-thirds Yellow Chartreuse One-third Cream (pony)
KING CHARLES	One pony Maraschino One jigger Tom Gin Three small lumps Ice (goblet) Fill with plain Soda; Fruit
KNICKERBINE	One-third sherry glass Crème de Rose One small Egg Yolk One-third Benedictine One-third Kümmel Three dashes Orange Bitters on top
KNICKERBOCKER	Juice one-half Lemon (Collins glass) One lump Sugar Two dashes Angostura Bitters One whole Lemon Peel One jigger Brandy Fill with plain chilled Soda

After a well known New York Club, then situated a few steps from the Waldorf, and supposed to have been originally compounded for members of that organization, as was the case with Knickerbocker Punch (*q. v.*).

LALLA ROOKH	One pony Vanilla (lemonade glass) One-half jigger Brandy One-half Jamaica Rum One-half spoon Sugar One tablespoon Whipped Cream Ice; shake well; strain
LAWYER'S REVENGE	One-fourth spoon Sugar Piece of Orange Peel One-half jigger Water; mix well Fill mixing glass with Ice Put over it jigger Port Wine Serve in star glass; add dash of Vichy
LEMONADE (*à la Taylor*)	Equal parts of Raspberry Syrup, Strawberry Syrup, Pineapple Syrup, Lemon Juice, Currant or Blackberry Syrup and Orange Juice, with small pieces of Banana Ice; fill glass with sparkling Water
LOENSKY	Two-thirds pony Russian Kümmel One-third Scotch Whiskey—no Ice
LUNE DE MIEL	One-third sherry glass White Cacao One-third Parfait d'Amour

Yolk of one Egg
One-third Kümmel Doré
Oftener drunk than correctly pronounced.

MAMIE GILROY	Juice one-half Lime (Collins glass) One dash Hostetter Bitters One jigger Scotch Whiskey One bottle chilled Club Soda
MAMIE TAYLOR	Juice one-half Lime (Collins glass) One jigger Scotch Whiskey One bottle imported Ginger Ale
MARGUERITE	One-half Lime (Collins glass) Lump Ice One jigger Tom Gin One imported Ginger Ale
MARTINIQUE	Two-thirds pony Benedictine One-third Cream—no Ice
MINCE PIE	Three-quarters pony Crème de Menthe One-quarter Brandy—no Ice

No mincemeat, no pie; only the brandy that was a standard mincemeat ingredient in those days.

MONT BLANC	One pony Orgeat Syrup (goblet) One jigger Absinthe White of one Egg Shake; strain; fill glass with chilled Seltzer
ORANGE BRANDY CUP	Cup an Orange; turn inside out Serve in glass with Brandy

ORANGE FLAMBÉE COGNAC	Cup an Orange Put rind in flat champagne glass, inside out Fill with shaved Ice Pour over it Cognac
ORANGE SMILE	Juice of two Oranges One Egg Enough Grenadine Syrup to color; frappé
PEACH BLOW	Juice one-quarter Lemon One-half spoon Sugar One-half Peach One jigger Tom Gin Ice; shake; strain; fill fizz glass from siphon
POMPIER	One-half jigger French Vermouth One-half jigger Crème de Cassis Ice; fill fizz or Collins glass with Seltzer

After the French term for "fireman"; but no French fireman would understand the usual orders that were given for it.

QUEEN CHARLOTTE	One pony Raspberry Syrup One jigger Claret Two lumps Ice (Collins glass) Fill with Lemon Soda; stir
ROBERT E. LEE	One dash Absinthe Juice of one Lime

	One drink of Scotch Whiskey Ice and shake (Collins glass) One bottle of Imported Ginger Ale
ROCK AND RYE	Two spoons Rock Candy Syrup One jigger Whiskey in whiskey glass Serve with small spoon
ROYAL SMILE	One-fourth Gordon Gin One-fourth Applejack One-fourth Grenadine One-fourth Lemon Juice; frappé
SABBATH CALM	One pony each, of Brandy, Port Wine and Black Coffee One Egg; one-half spoon Sugar Fill two-thirds with Cream Shake; strain into goblet; Nutmeg
SHANDYGAFF (pitcher)	One bottle Ginger Ale One bottle Bass Ale; mix
SHERRY AND EGG	One-fourth claret glass Sherry One Egg Fill glass with Sherry
SHERRY CHICKEN	Egg-nog; made with Sherry
SINGLE STANDARD	Rickey, made with Whiskey, instead of Gin, and served in goblet

This belongs to the same period, and has an origin similar to that of Double Standard Sour and Free Silver Fizz.

| SMALL BEER | Three-fourths pony Crème de Cacao
One-fourth Cream |

SNOW BALL   White of one Egg
                  One-half spoon Sugar (Collins glass)
                  One jigger Medford Rum
                  Shake; strain; fill with chilled Gin-
                      ger Ale

SOOTHER   One-half spoon Sugar
                  Juice one-half Lemon
                  One pony Brandy
                  One pony Jamaica Rum
                  One-half pony Curaçao
                  One spoon pure Apple Juice
                  Ice; shake; strain into goblet

STONE FENCE   Two lumps Ice (fizz glass)
                  One jigger Whiskey
                  Fill glass with Cider (spoon)

SUISETTE   Break one Egg in glass
                  Juice of one Lemon
                  One-third jigger Italian Vermouth
                  Two-thirds jigger Brandy
                  Two dashes Absinthe
                  One spoon Sugar
                  Frappé and fill lemonade glass from
                      siphon

SUISSESSE   Three-quarters jigger Absinthe
                  One-fourth pony Anisette
                  Ice; shake well; strain; fill star glass
                      from siphon

SUNSHINE   Juice one-half each, Lime and Orange
                  White of one Egg

	Jigger of Gin or Whiskey Fizz with Carbonic (lemonade glass)
SYMPHONY OF MOIST JOY	Wine-glass of shaved Ice One-fourth each, Crème de Rose, Yellow Chartreuse, Crème de Menthe and Cognac; Berries on top
THREE- QUARTER	One-third each; Yellow Chartreuse, Curaçao and Brandy (sherry glass)
TOM COLLINS	Juice of one-half Lemon One-half spoon Sugar One jigger Tom Gin Ice; shake; strain; fill with plain Soda
WHISKEY AND MINT	Three sprigs Mint One-half lump Sugar, dissolved; press Mint lightly One jigger Whiskey; Ice
WHISKEY AND TANSY	Three leaves of Tansy, or a pony of Tansy Mixture One jigger Whiskey
WHISKEY DAISY	Juice of one-half Lemon One-half spoon Sugar One pony Raspberry Syrup One jigger Whiskey Ice; shake; strain; fill from siphon
WHISKEY FIX	One lump Sugar One jigger Whiskey

Brandy Fix made similarly. Some added one-fourth of a Lemon and one-half Water.

VELVET — One pint Wine (Champagne)
One pint Dublin Stout

VICTORY — Equal parts of Irish Whiskey, Hol-
SWIZZLE — land Gin and Jamaica Rum, with
juice of one-half Lemon; frappé
Named in honor either of Dewey's victory at Manila
Bay or of the Battle of Santiago. Swizzles were first
imported from Cuba by American naval officers.

WALDORF — Apricotine and Lime Juice, equal
FRAPPÉ — parts; frappé

WARD EIGHT — Whiskey Sour, with Grenadine

WHISPERS — Equal parts in goblet, Whiskey,
OF THE FROST — Sherry, and Port Wine
Add Sugar, to taste
Fruit well; Ice

WIDOW'S KISS — One-quarter sherry glass Parfait
d'Amour
One-quarter Yellow Chartreuse
One-quarter Benedictine
White of one Egg, beaten, on top
On the last, put slice of Strawberry
Just why the author of this drink should ascribe so
many tastes to the osculation of some gentleman's relict,
or who was the widow whose kiss was thus commemo-
rated, it has been impossible to establish. One could only
suggest that someone with an inquiring mind might
catch a widow and experiment with direct labial contact.

NON-ALCOHOLIC

CIDER NOG | One-half spoon Sugar
One Egg
Shake well; fill with chilled Cider
Stir well; serve with napkin

DUMMY DAISY | One pony Raspberry Syrup
Juice one Lime (lemonade glass)
One-half spoon Sugar; Seltzer
Ice

EGG FLIP | One-fourth spoon Sugar
One Egg
Fill two-thirds goblet with Milk
Ice; shake; strain

EGG LEMONADE | Juice one Lemon
One-half spoon Sugar
Fill with Water
One Egg
Ice; shake well; strain

EGG PHOSPHATE | One Egg
One-half spoon Sugar
Three dashes Acid Phosphate
Shake well; fill with chilled
Soda

FLORIDA SPECIAL | One drink Orange Juice
One lump Ice
Split of Ginger Ale

GRASSHOPPER   One-half Lemon Juice
                     One-half Orange Juice
                     One whole Egg
                     One-half teaspoon Sugar; Ice

HORSE'S NECK   Whole of a Lemon Peel (Collins
                        glass)
                     Ice; one bottle Ginger Ale

LEMONADE, PLAIN   Juice of one Lemon
                     One-half spoonful Sugar
                     Fill with plain Water
                     Ice; shake; fruit

LEMON   Three dashes Acid Phosphate
PHOSPHATE   One spoon Lemon Juice
                     Fill with Lemon Soda; Stir

LEMON SQUASH   Muddle one Lemon (Collins
                        glass)
                     One-half spoon Sugar
                     Fill with plain Soda; Ice; stir

MINT COOLER   Three or four sprigs of Mint
                     Two lumps Ice (Collins glass)
                     One bottle Ginger Ale

ORANGEADE   Juice of one and one-half
                        Oranges
                     One-quarter spoon Sugar
                     Fill two-thirds with Water
                     Ice; shake; strain

ORANGE LILY   Juice of two Oranges
                     White of one Egg; Frappé

ORANGE PHOSPHATE	Juice one-half Orange Two dashes Syrup Three dashes Acid Phosphate Ice; stir; fill with plain Soda
PRAIRIE CHICKEN	See PRAIRIE COCKTAIL
SARATOGA COOLER	Whole rind of Lemon Two or three lumps Ice (Collins glass) Fill one-half with Sarsaparilla One-half with Imported Ginger Ale
SELTZER LEMONADE	Juice of one Lemon One-half spoon Sugar Ice; fill with Seltzer; stir slowly

Also the following "cocktails" (*q. v.*): Ammonia, Cider, Mountain, Soda and Prairie.

B.

AMENDMENTS

DRINKS FROM OTHER CLIMES

---•---

1. MOSTLY WITH FRENCH SPIRIT

---•---

FOR reasons earlier elaborated, the art of invention, as applied to cocktails, suffered in this country a sort of hiatus during the so-called Dry Era. Americans who traveled abroad became aware that determined efforts were being made by sympathetic foreigners to keep the American School of Drinking alive—with amendments. All over Europe, in particular, visitors from this side were assured that cocktails answering to all the old familiar names would come when called, if asked for in the proper places. Many kinds were called for, but after some sampling, few varieties were chosen again.

So far as I have been able to ascertain, Europe, during the Dark Interim, produced just one new cocktail that Americans took to and adopted. I first came across it in Rome. My host there, Commendatore Giulio Gelardi, General Manager of the Hotel Excelsior, did not, however, claim the Side-Car for Italy, and Mussolini himself was silent on the subject. Americans who make their homes abroad and so have been able to watch the March of Invention over there, trace its origin to the Ritz Bar, in Paris. The correct formula:

SIDE-CAR   One-third Lemon or Lime Juice
COCKTAIL   One-third Cointreau
           One-third Brandy

The Side-Car is somewhat reminiscent of the Stinger, as New York knew it before the War, except that the Stinger had no fruit juice in it, and needed none, having a strong mint flavor. In English fiction dealing with the Malay States, the characters seem to be forever calling for a drink of similar name. One can scarcely read a page of W. Somerset Maugham's recently published tales without being tripped up by an order to a menial to "stengah-up" his thirsty boss or the latter's guests, who then take time off to drink. "Undoubtedly," one man was heard to say who had got as near Singapore as Paterson, N. J., "that was where we got the Stinger."

He was wrong, but not until one turned up a friend who had a friend just back from Singapore was it established that "stengah" is Malay for "half." It came to mean a drink because it seemed the easiest way for a Malay servant to gather what a Britisher wanted when in need of a half-size "spot" of his favorite beverage. So that, when Mr. Maugham's characters call for stengahs, what they get are small Scotch-and-Sodas.

The pre-prohibition Stinger was thus composed:

STINGER   Two-thirds Brandy
          One-third White Crème de Menthe
          Frappé, and serve in cocktail glass

In the Stinger that now comes back to us from France, the Brandy and the White Mint mingle in equal proportions.

From Paris too have come since Repeal a number of

good recipes based on Brandy, or Cognac, which is France's best contribution to the category of Ardent Drink. Some of the recipes were known in the United States before the War. As all contain Brandy, I have classed them as

BRANDY POTATIONS

BRANDY AND SODA	One wine-glass Brandy One-third shaved Ice Fill with plain Soda Water
BRANDY CHAMPAGNE PUNCH	Ice in Punch bowl Small glass of Brandy Liqueur glass Maraschino Liqueur glass Benedictine Barspoon pulverized Sugar One quart Champagne One pint aerated Water Use plenty of Fruit; mix well

BRANDY
CIDER NECTAR
(pitcher)
	Pony of Brandy
	One quart Cider
	One glass Sherry
	One bottle Soda Water
	Juice of half Lemon
	Sweeten to taste
	Grate Nutmeg on top
	Add sprig of Verbena and dash
	   of Pineapple Extract, or few
	   spoons Pineapple Juice
	Ice; mix; strain

BRANDY COBBLER — One-half tablespoon Sugar in Water
One dash Maraschino (tall glass)
One jigger Brandy
One slice Orange, quartered
Fill with Ice; stir well; dress with fruits and serve with straws

BRANDY COCKTAIL — Fill glass two-thirds with Ice
Three dashes Syrup
Three dashes Angostura Bitters
One dash Orange Bitters
Fill glass with Brandy
Twist piece of Lemon Peel

BRANDY COCKTAIL (OLD-FASHIONED) — One lump Sugar (whiskey glass)
Crush in dash of aerated Water
One dash Orange Bitters
One cube Ice
Piece of Lemon Peel
One jigger Brandy; stir (spoon)

BRANDY COLLINS — Fill Collins glass one-third with shaved Ice
One wine-glass Brandy
Fill with aerated Water

BRANDY DAISY — Fill shaker half-full of Ice
Three dashes Syrup
Three dashes Curaçao
Three dashes Lemon Juice

One wine-glass Brandy
Shake; strain; fill with aerated
Water

BRANDY FIZZ

One wine-glass Brandy
Three dashes Lemon Juice
One teaspoon powdered Sugar
Ice; fill with aerated Water;
stir

BRANDY FLIP

Fill shaker half-full of Ice
One Egg
One-half tablespoon Sugar
One wine-glass Brandy
Shake; strain; grate Nutmeg on
top

BRANDY
MORNING GLORY

Two dashes each, of Syrup,
Lemon Juice, Curaçao and
Absinthe
One-half jigger Brandy
One-half jigger Rye Whiskey
Shake; strain; fill glass with
aerated Water

GEORGIA
MINT JULEP

Three-quarters wine-glass
Brandy
Three-quarters wine-glass Peach
Brandy
Teaspoon powdered Sugar
Twelve sprigs fresh Mint
Place Mint in tall glass; add
Sugar, dissolved in Water;

add the Brandies; fill glass
with shaved Ice. Do not crush
Mint

MOSELLE CUP
(pitcher)

One pint Moselle
One pint aerated Water
One glass Sherry
One pony Brandy
One pony Anisette
Three thin slices Pineapple
Rind of one Lemon; sweeten to
    taste
Ice; fresh Mint on top

RHINE WINE CUP
(pitcher)

Two liqueur glasses Brandy on
    cracked Ice
One liqueur glass Orange Cura-
    çao
One liqueur glass Maraschino
One quart Rhine Wine
One-half pint aerated Water
Fruits; piece Cucumber Peel
Several sprigs fresh Mint; mix
    well

SAUTERNE CUP
(pitcher)

Two ponies Brandy on cracked
    Ice
One pony Orange Curaçao
One pony Maraschino
One quart Sauterne
Half-pint aerated Water; Fruits
Piece of Cucumber Peel; fresh
    Mint; mix

2. *CUBAN CONCOCTIONS*

It was during trips to the West Indies, during the last dozen years or more, that many Americans learned a good deal about good cocktails and other mixed drinks that was not always practicable either at home or in Europe. In such beverages they often found solace, cures for home-sickness and new tastes and flavors of delightful charm, not to mention considerable potency. Most of such travelers found their ideas of what may make good drinks first broadened in Havana.

COCKTAILS

From Will P. Taylor, manager of the Hotel National, in Havana, who stuck at his post all through the recent local disturbances, which included a bombardment of his hotel, I have obtained the choicest Cuban Rum recipes. Out of compliment to Mr. Taylor, who was last resident manager of the Old Waldorf-Astoria, is placed at the head of this list the distinctive cocktail which at his hotel is also called a Daiquiri, or a Bacardi. It is served in a tall glass, instead of the flat Champagne type usual at Havana bars, and to my taste is at its best when white Bacardi is used. The recipe:

NATIONAL   Equal parts of Bacardi and Pineapple
                Juice
            Squeeze of Lemon
            Dash of Apricot Brandy
            Ice; shake; strain

Other Havana recipes follow. Cocktails should be shaken except where stirring is specified.

BACARDI DUBONNET	One-half jigger Bacardi One-half jigger Dubonnet Juice of half Lime One teaspoonful Grenadine; shaved Ice in glass
BACARDI OLD-FASHIONED	One dash Angostura Bitters Two dashes Orange Bitters One lump Sugar, dissolved in two spoonfuls Water One jigger Bacardi Serve in "old-fashioned" glass Dress with Fruit and fresh Mint
BACARDI VERMOUTH (Dry)	Half wine-glass Bacardi Half wine-glass French Vermouth Shaved Ice (Stir)
BACARDI VERMOUTH (Sweet)	Half wine-glass Bacardi Half wine-glass Italian Vermouth Shaved Ice (Stir)
BERRY	One-third mixed Orange and Pineapple Juice Two-thirds Bacardi Dash of Grenadine
BISHOP	Juice of half a Lime One-half barspoon Sugar Two-thirds Bacardi One-third Claret

BOWMAN BACARDI	Crush small spoonful Sugar Three sprigs Mint One-third Orange Juice Two-thirds Bacardi

    Named after the late John McEntee Bowman, American hotel man, who was the first to introduce modern American hotel-keeping into Havana and who, making the acquaintance of Bacardi on its native heath, probably did more to popularize it among Americans than any other one person.

COUNTRY CLUB	One-half Bacardi One-half French Vermouth Dash of Orange Curaçao
CUBAN BLOSSOM	One-half Orange Juice One-half Bacardi Dash of Maraschino
CUBAN BRONX	One-fourth Orange Juice One-fourth Bacardi One-fourth French Vermouth One-fourth Italian Vermouth
CUBAN CLOVER CLUB	Two dashes Grenadine Juice one Lime Dash of Orange Juice White of one Egg One drink of Bacardi (white wine-glass)
CUBAN CORONATION	One-third Bacardi One-third French Vermouth One-third Dubonnet (Stir)

CUBAN LIBERAL	Two-thirds Bacardi One-third Italian Vermouth One dash Amer Picon (Stir)
CUBAN MANHATTAN	One-half Bacardi One-half Italian Vermouth A few drops Angostura Bitters
CUBAN PRINCE	One-half Bacardi One-half Italian Vermouth Dash of white Crème de Menthe (Stir)
CUBAN SIDE-CAR	One-third Lemon or Lime Juice One-third Bacardi One-third Triple Sec or Cointreau
CUBAN ROSE	One-third Orange Juice Two-thirds Bacardi Dash of Grenadine
DAIQUIRI	One part Bacardi Juice of half a Lime One barspoon powdered Sugar

Note: The order of adding ingredients is important. Personal preference dictates serving the cocktail with finely shaved ice in the glass.

DOROTHY GISH	One-third mixed Orange and Pineapple Juice Two-thirds Bacardi Dash of Apricot Brandy
ELIXIR	Juice of half a Lime One-half barspoon Sugar

Two-thirds Bacardi Elixir
One-third Bacardi

FOUR DOLLARS   One-third Bacardi
One-third French Vermouth
One-third Italian Vermouth

GRAPEFRUIT   One-third Grapefruit Juice
BLOSSOM   Two-thirds Bacardi
Three dashes Maraschino

GRENADINE   One jigger Bacardi
One teaspoon Grenadine
Juice of half Lime (shaved Ice in
glass)

HAVANA OPERA   One-half Bacardi
One-half Dubonnet
Dash of Lemon Juice
Twist Orange Peel on top

HAVANA SMILE   One-half Bacardi
One-half Italian Vermouth
A little Sugar
A little Lime Juice

HIGH-STEPPER   One-third Orange Juice
Two-thirds Bacardi
Dash of Apricot Brandy

ISLE OF PINES   One-half teaspoon Sugar
One-third Grapefruit Juice
Two-thirds Bacardi

MARY PICKFORD	One-third Pineapple Juice Two-thirds Bacardi Dash of Grenadine
MENENDEZ	One-third mixed Orange and Pine- apple Juice One-third Bacardi One-third French Vermouth Dash of Apricot Brandy
PARADISE	Two-thirds Bacardi One-third Apricot Brandy
PRESIDENTE	One-half Bacardi One-half French Vermouth One dash Grenadine (shake or stir) Twist Orange Peel on top
SUNSHINE	One-third Pineapple Juice One-third Bacardi One-third French Vermouth Dash of Grenadine
YACHT CLUB	Two-thirds Bacardi One-third Italian Vermouth Dash of Apricot Brandy (Stir)

FIZZES AND FLIPS

BACARDI FIZZ	Juice of half Lemon One barspoon Sugar One jigger Bacardi; Ice; shake

Strain into fizz glass; fill from
siphon

GOLDEN FIZZ   Juice of half Lemon
                       One barspoon Sugar
                       Yolk of one Egg
                       One jigger Bacardi; Ice; shake
                       Strain into fizz glass; fill from
                       siphon

PINEAPPLE   One barspoon Sugar
FIZZ   One jigger Pineapple Juice
                       One jigger Bacardi; Ice; shake
                       Strain into fizz glass; fill from
                       siphon

ROYAL FIZZ   Juice of half Lemon
                       One barspoon Sugar
                       One jigger Bacardi
                       One Egg; Ice; shake
                       Strain into fizz glass and fill from
                       siphon

SILVER FIZZ   Juice of half Lemon
                       One barspoon Sugar
                       One jigger Bacardi
                       White of one Egg; Ice; shake
                       Strain into fizz glass; fill from
                       siphon

SUNSHINE FIZZ   Juice of half Lemon
                       Juice of half an Orange
                       White of one Egg
                       One jigger Bacardi; Ice; shake

Strain into fizz glass; fill from siphon

BACARDI FLIP
One barspoon Sugar
One Egg
One jigger Bacardi; Ice; shake
Strain into a Delmonico glass

ORANGE JUICE FLIP
One barspoon Sugar
One Egg
One drink Orange Juice
One drink Bacardi; Ice; shake
Serve in a fizz glass

MISCELLANEOUS

BACARDI BUCK
Two lumps of Ice in high-ball glass
Juice of half Lime
One jigger Bacardi
"Split" of Ginger Ale

BACARDI COLLINS
Juice of one Lime
One spoonful Sugar
One jigger Bacardi; Ice; shake
Strain into Collins glass in which are three lumps Ice
Fill with Club Soda
Stir with spoon

BACARDI COOLER
One lump Ice in Collins glass
One jigger Bacardi
Plenty of fresh Mint
"Split" of Ginger Ale

BACARDI DAISY	Juice of one Lime Two dashes Grenadine One jigger Bacardi; Ice; shake Strain into goblet filled with shaved Ice Dash of Yellow Chartreuse on top Dress with Fruit and Mint
BACARDI EGG-NOG	One spoonful Sugar One wine-glass Bacardi One Egg; one glass Milk Ice; shake well Strain into Collins glass Grate little Nutmeg on top
BACARDI MILK PUNCH	One glass hot Milk One tablespoon Sugar Pinch of grated Nutmeg Yolk of one Egg One jigger Bacardi Now, beat up thoroughly the yolk of Egg with the Sugar; add Milk, next Bacardi, next Nutmeg. Mix thoroughly
BACARDI PLANTERS' PUNCH	Juice of one Lime One barspoon Sugar One jigger Bacardi; shake Strain into goblet Fill with shaved Ice Decorate with Fruit and Mint

BACARDI PLUS   One pony Bacardi
Two dashes Crème de Cacao
One dash Anisette
Shaved Ice; stir; strain

BACARDI
RICKEY   Two lumps Ice in high-ball glass
Juice of half Lime
One jigger Bacardi
"Split" of aerated Water

BACARDI SOUR   Juice of half Lime
One barspoon Sugar
One jigger Bacardi; Ice; shake
Strain into a Delmonico glass
Dress with Fruit

BACARDI
TODDY   Crush half lump Sugar with little
Water in "old-fashioned" glass
One lump Ice
One jigger Bacardi
One Lemon Peel (Stir)

BRUNSWICK
SOUR   Juice of half Lime
Barspoon Sugar
Jigger Bacardi; Ice; shake
Strain into Delmonico glass
Dash of Claret on top; Fruit

CUBA LIBRE   Half portions of Bacardi and Coca
Cola

GROG   Two quarts Bacardi
Two pounds Sugar

Two quarts Formosa Oolong Tea
When serving, dilute one-half with
    very hot Water in which Sugar
    has been dissolved and put slice
    of Lemon in glass

MOJITO   Same as Bacardi Rickey, with little
                    Sugar and few sprigs of Mint
                    added

MORNING   One spoonful Sugar
STAR   One Egg
                One-half jigger Bacardi
                One-half jigger Port Wine
                One glass Milk; Ice; shake well
                Strain into a Collins glass
                Grate little Nutmeg on top

NIGHTCAP   One-third Orange Curaçao
                Two-thirds Bacardi
                Yolk of one Egg; Ice; shake
                Strain into white wine-glass

PEACH   Teaspoon powdered Sugar (tall
                    glass) dissolved in Water
                Fresh crushed Mint
                Juice of two Lemons
                Three jiggers Bacardi
                Layer of shaved Ice in glass
                One whole pitted fresh Peach
                Another layer shaved Ice
                Dress with Mint; serve with straws

3. JAMAICAN JOLLIFIERS

Rum, Rum, Jamaica Rum!
Who in thy praise is dumb?
The strong, the weak, the gay, the glum—
All call thee good, Jamaica Rum!
—Old Song

It is recorded in Rupert Hughes—or somewhere—that the Father of His Country so highly esteemed Jamaica Rum that he once swapped a perfectly healthy negro slave for a cask of it. That, somehow, makes one recall a famous cartoon of the late Homer Davenport's—Roosevelt with Uncle Sam tapping him on the shoulder and saying, "He's good enough for me!"

As a matter of fact, George Washington did not stand alone. Many of our Revolutionary and colonial fathers knew Jamaica Rum and liked it. The Pilgrim Fathers knew rum, or came to know it, and when swallowed it seemed to go down well with the Puritan conscience. For many years rum was one of the products of New England. Perhaps Plymouth Rock and Massachusetts Bay were originally attracted to it by its ancient name.

When Englishmen first discovered what could be done with cane sugar in Barbados, rum was known as "Kill-Devill," and under that guise it made its first appearance in English literature. It was said to be a sure cure for "Blue Devils." Soon it was rechristened with the Devonshire name of "Rumbullion," meaning "a great tumult"— probably a case of swapping cause for effect. In time it became the most famous product of Jamaica, its manufacture in that Island having attained such a degree of perfection by 1788 that John Hunter, a British army physician, after a careful observation of its effects, acquitted Jamaica Rum of any complicity in the ills that befell British soldiers stationed there; in substance, Hunter declared it had no stain on its character, and that it could be drunk with absolute impunity. Thereupon the British navy adopted it as its own. Still, certain British lexicographers maintain that "Rum" is an American word, coined generations before the British acquired the habit of abbreviation, from the good old Devonshire "Rumbullion."

It is to Mr. T. G. S. Hooke, for many years assistant manager of the old Hotel Belmont, in New York, but for some years past general manager of the Myrtlebank Hotel in Kingston, Jamaica, and the Tichfield, in Port Antonio, that I am indebted for the following collection of the best cocktails and other local concoctions in which the most-famed product of Jamaica finds favor among visitors from northern latitudes.

COCKTAILS

Note: Ingredients should be added in order named. Shake except where stirring is specified. Cocktails should usually be strained.

CHINESE

Fill bar glass half full of Ice
One or two dashes Angostura
Three dashes Maraschino
Three dashes Curaçao
Three dashes Grenadine
Half glass Jamaica Rum (Stir)
Add Cherry; squeeze Lemon Peel on top

DOLORES
Half glass Sherry
Quarter glass Jamaica Rum
One-eighth glass Dubonnet
One-eighth glass Orange Juice
Dash of aromatic Pepper

FLAPPER
One-half Jamaica Rum
One-half French Vermouth
Two dashes Angostura Bitters
Sweeten to taste
Serve with Maraschino Cherry
and slice of Orange

GRENADE
Half glass Grenadine
Quarter glass French Vermouth
Quarter glass Jamaica Rum

HONEY DEW
Eight parts Jamaica Rum
Two parts Gin
Two parts Vermouth
Two parts Water
Juice of fresh Lime or Lemon,
sweetened
Crushed Ice in glass (Stir)

JAMAICA
KNICKERBOCKER
Three-fourths Jamaica Rum
One-fourth Orange, Lemon or
Lime Juice
Two dashes Grenadine
Crushed Ice in glass (Stir)

JAMAICA
ORANGE
Half glass Jamaica Rum
Quarter glass Italian Vermouth
Quarter glass sweet Orange Juice

Pinch of powdered Cinnamon

JAMAICA RUM

Half glass Jamaica Rum
Quarter glass Gin
One teaspoon Grenadine
Juice of one Lime or Lemon

KINGSTON

Half glass Jamaica Rum
Quarter glass Kümmel
Quarter glass strained Orange Juice
Dash of Pimento Dram

LIFE-SAVER

One-half Jamaica Rum
One-half Orange Juice

MAREE

Half glass Jamaica Rum
Half glass sweetened Lime or Lemon Juice
Dash of Bitters
Bit of grated Nutmeg

PLANTER'S

One-third Jamaica Rum
One-third Orange Juice
One-third Lime or Lemon Juice
Serve with crushed Ice

QUEEN ELIZABETH

Five parts Jamaica Rum
One part Lime or Lemon Juice
One part Grenadine

RUM AND FRUIT

Half glass Jamaica Rum
Quarter glass sweet Fruit Juice
One teaspoon Kümmel
One teaspoon Benedictine

Two teaspoons Lime or Lemon
Juice

RUM CRUSTA

Prepare glass thus:
Moisten edge in Lemon, dip in
powdered Sugar
Cut ends from a Lemon; peel rest
like an apple; put rind inside
glass so that it lines the latter
Fill shaker with Ice
Three dashes plain Syrup
Three dashes Maraschino
Two dashes Angostura Bitters
Juice of quarter Lime or Lemon
Half glass Jamaica Rum
Shake; strain into glass
Fruit; serve with spoon

SEPTEMBER
MORN
(Jamaica)

White of one Egg
Juice of half Lime or Lemon
One teaspoon Grenadine
Half glass Jamaica Rum

TEA TIME

Half glass Jamaica Rum
Half glass cold Tea
Dash of Lime or Lemon Juice
Sweeten as desired

VOLCANO

Heaping teaspoon granulated
Sugar, dissolved in Water
One-half glass Jamaica Rum
Juice of Lime or Lemon (Stir)
Fill with crushed Ice and stir again

WINTER

Two-thirds glass Jamaica Rum
Juice of one Lime or Lemon
Sugar to taste
Teaspoon of Ginger Brandy and
    Pimento Liqueur
Two dashes Angostura Bitters

PUNCHES

CARIBBEAN
FISH-HOUSE

Two quarts Jamaica Rum
One quart Brandy
Four ounces powdered Sugar
Juice of twelve Lemons
Liqueur glass Maraschino
Large wine-glass Peach Brandy
Ice; mix well; Fruit

COLD RUM AND
BRANDY

One-third pint Lime or Lemon
    Juice
Twelve ounces Sugar, dissolved in
    Water
Half pint Brandy
One gill Peach Brandy
One gill Jamaica Rum
Two and one-half pints Ice Water
Add Ice; mix

HOT RUM

One pint Jamaica Rum
Half pint Brandy
Half wine-glass Kümmel
Half wine-glass Benedictine
Peel of one Lemon
Peel of one Orange
One sliced Orange

One sliced Lemon or Lime
Sweeten to taste
Add three pints boiling Water
Stir up well

JAMAICA MILK   Fill shaker with Ice
One tablespoon plain Syrup
Quarter glass Jamaica Rum
Quarter glass Brandy
Fill with rich Milk
Shake; strain; serve in tumbler
with grated Nutmeg on top

JAMAICA PUNCH   Fill shaker with Ice
One tablespoon plain Syrup
Juice of half Lime or Lemon
Half glass Jamaica Rum; shake;
strain

MISSISSIPPI
PUNCH
One small glass Brandy
One-half glass Jamaica Rum
One-half glass Bourbon Whiskey
One and one-half tablespoons
Sugar
Mix well; pour into tumbler; fill
with shaved Ice; add small
pieces of Orange or other Fruits

MYERS'
PLANTER'S
PUNCH
One part Lime Juice
Two parts Sugar
Three parts Jamaica Rum
Four parts Water and Ice
Dash of Angostura Bitters
Shake well

OLD NAVY
PUNCH

One quart Jamaica Rum
One pint Brandy
Three pints Champagne
Two-thirds pint Lemon Juice
One and one-half pounds Sugar
Juice of three Oranges
One gill Peach Brandy

MISCELLANEOUS

BLACK STRIPE

Dissolve teaspoon Honey in little
   hot Water
Cool; add three lumps Ice
Half glass Jamaica Rum
Fill with cold Water
Grate Nutmeg on top
(Same as a hot drink made by
   using boiling Water)

CLARET CUP
AUX CERISES

Crush pound of red or black Cher-
   ries
Cover with quarter bottle Jamaica
   Rum
Let stand several hours in cool
   place
Add two bottles Claret (or three)
One sliced Orange; thin Lemon
   Peel
Ice; add aerated Water

EGG-NOG
BALTIMORE

One fresh Egg
One teaspoon plain Syrup
Quarter glass Madeira

Quarter glass Jamaica Rum
Fresh Milk
Ice; shake; strain into tumbler
Grated Nutmeg on top

EGG-NOG JAMAICA	Fill shaker with Ice One fresh Egg One teaspoon plain Syrup Half glass Jamaica Rum Fill with rich Milk Shake well; strain into tumbler Grated Nutmeg on top
EGG-NOG MYERS	Fill shaker with Ice One fresh Egg One teaspoon plain Syrup Quarter glass Brandy Quarter glass Jamaica Rum Fill with rich Milk Shake well; strain into tumbler Grated Nutmeg on top
HOT SPICED RUM	Two teaspoons Sugar, dissolved in boiling Water Half glass Jamaica Rum Piece of Butter, walnut-size Teaspoon mixed Spices (Cinnamon, Cloves, etc.) Fill glass with boiling Water Slice of Lemon on top
JAMAICA COLD TEA	Make Tea; before it becomes bitter, strain into jug and let grow cold.

Put in tumblers, one for each
   person
One teaspoon Prune Syrup
One teaspoon Curaçao
One teaspoon Jamaica Rum
Ice; sweeten to taste; fill glasses
   from jug

JAMAICA   Two lumps Ice
HIGH-BALL   Half cocktail glass Jamaica Rum
                 Fill from siphon
                 Add slice of Lime or Lemon

JAMAICA JULEP   Mash half dozen sprigs fresh
                    Mint with Sugar and Water
                 Strain into bar glass; Ice
                 Half cocktail glass Jamaica Rum
                 Shake; strain into glass thus pre-
                    pared:
                 Tumbler or balloon glass, filled
                    with shaved Ice; three sprigs
                    fresh Mint, dipped in powdered
                    Sugar, and leaves upward
                 Now decorate drink with Berries,
                    Pineapple, Banana, Orange or
                    other fruit

JAMAICA   Juice of six Oranges
ORANGE CUP   Half pint Water
                 Sweeten; put in jug with
                 Half tumbler Jamaica Rum
                 Two teaspoons Essence of Orange

Let jug stand on Ice one hour
Serve, filling glasses with aerated
Water

**JAMAICA
SWIZZLE**

One pint Jamaica Rum (tall
pitcher, or jug)
Juice of six Limes or Lemons
Six small cubes Ice
Four spoons Sugar
Few sprigs fresh Mint
Use swizzle stick, rolling top be-
tween hands until mixture
froths and outside of pitcher
frosts

RUM-ADE

Two tablespoons Jamaica Rum
in glass of Lemonade

RUM DAISY

Dissolve little Sugar in Water in
shaker; Ice
Juice of half Lime or Lemon
Quarter glass Curaçao or Yellow
Chartreuse
Half glass Jamaica Rum
Shake; strain; decorate with fruit;
serve with spoon

RUM RICKEY

Two lumps Ice in tumbler or tall
glass
Squeeze half Lime or Lemon
Half cocktail glass Jamaica Rum
Fill with chilled aerated Water;
serve with spoon

RUM SANGAREE   Spoonful Sugar, dissolved in small wine-glass Water
Pour into large tumbler or tall glass
Fill up with Jamaica Rum and Water in desired proportions
One or two lumps Ice; serve with spoon

RUM SOUR   Fill shaker with Ice
One teaspoon plain Syrup
Juice of half Lime or Lemon
Half cocktail glass Jamaica Rum
Shake; strain; splash of Soda Water on top
Fruit

RUM TODDY (cold)   Dissolve Sugar in Water in small tumbler
Ice
Half cocktail glass Jamaica Rum

RUM TODDY (hot)   Dissolve Sugar in hot Water in small tumbler
Half cocktail glass Jamaica Rum
Slice of Lemon on top

TEA COBBLER   One teaspoon plain Syrup in shaker
Teaspoon Pineapple Syrup, or Curaçao
Half cocktail glass Jamaica Rum
Ice; shake; strain into tumbler

filled with cracked Ice; decorate
with sliced Fruit; serve with
straws and spoon

WHITE LION   Juice of half Lime or Lemon
Quarter glass Raspberry Syrup
Quarter glass Curaçao
Half glass Jamaica Rum
Shake, strain into tumbler filled
with shaved Ice
Fruit

THE OLD WALDORF BAR
1897–1919

NOT far from the spot where the Indian chief who sold Peter Minuit the Island of Manhattan coined the expression, "Here's how!" when he tackled the bottle of rum that the crafty Dutchman threw after his twenty-four dollars to bind the bargain; not far from that spirituous spot, in later years, arose a mighty hotel. In one of its great halls, disciples, if not descendants, of the noble red man were wont to assemble every afternoon, and to preface, as well as conclude, with his utterance on that memorable occasion, deals which caused the original New York real estate speculation to dwindle to the proportions of a fly-speck.

What some of those men did, under the influence of a just-ended session of the Stock Exchange, of the news-ticker that kept discharging its tape into a waste-basket, and possibly—and probably—of what was dispensed in that hall by a dozen talented bartenders, helped make American history. Men staked fortunes there; they formed pools; they plotted to corner markets. For years the names of certain of them made the first page of the newspapers almost every day. They were, in their way, giants, and they took their ease in a Gargantuan way.

Many of that noble army of gallant drinkers I knew by name; many others I knew by sight. The majority have gone. The great hall where they exercised elbows and appeased arid appetites every day, some of them for more than twenty years, ceased to function one dark day in June, 1919. While the light holds, let me try to recreate it, and to limn the shapes of some of those who went surging in and out, while, above the roar of conversation and the chatter of the ticker, the air was rent with calls of "Same here!" and "Here's how!"

On the walls are a few paintings—expensive-looking. Here and there is a piece of massive, if not always ornamental, statuary. In one corner stands a great rectangular counter, behind which a dozen men in white coats are busy all afternoon and evening ministering to an endless array of thirsts.

The crowd surges in. Everyone struggles to get a foothold on a brass rail that runs around the bottom of the bar. Sometimes the gang is ten deep, all pressing toward that common goal. On every face is written strong resolve. Each man pushes forward until some drinker who has been monopolizing a coveted spot falls or otherwise gives way; and then, with something like a shout, the late-comer, if he is a good squirmer or ducker, wiggles into the place thus vacated, to claim the drink he yelled for while still a Sheridan's ride away.

It should be stressed that the scene described was typical only of hours when the room was overcrowded, as it frequently was toward six o'clock of an afternoon, when men would come in who acted as if they had only one aim in life, and that was to get outside of a drink, and with no delay. Frequently, as intimated, their chances improved when some "tank" at the barside had filled to overflowing and had to be either carried or led away.

But, be it also emphasized, that Bar was not regarded as a place of "ill-repute." In its early days, particularly, men of the highest reputation frequented it; some never went from their offices downtown to their homes without calling in for at least an appetizer—or something to make them forget the worry or turmoil of the day's work. Anybody could look in, and most every man who entered the Waldorf-Astoria in those days did look, at least once. It was known all over the country; in mining camps from Mexico to Alaska, it evoked recollections of tastes and odors that parched many a throat. As a matter of fact, its fame was world-wide.

Visitors to the Old Waldorf during its latter days found difficulty, did they seek to recreate the picture of that great hall where Bacchus so long drew his greatest throngs of pilgrims and devotees, and where such, in turn, drew inspiration of the widest spirituous variety. On the spot mostly occupied by the great bar counter, a humidor had been built, and ex-tanks who came and looked through a once popular doorway often could not remember which was the proper direction to cast their sighs of regret. The back entrance from the lobby—past the telephone switchboard—with its inviting facilities for gentlemen whose capacity had been stretched, had been closed, and here young women armed with pencils and typewriters were taking dictation from industrial, financial, railway and legal magnates, so classed. Across the room and against a partition were desks for various managerial heads and factotums. And when one's eye reached that partition they had embraced only half of the room where for decades the thirsty had libationed from eight in the morning until closing time. The second part of the great oak-wainscoted hall had been converted into a bus station, and there one bought tickets for Montclair, the Oranges, and other points in New Jersey, or else for New Haven and other way stations to Boston.

Some of the decorations of the temple remained. For example, two great Egyptian-like bronze figures still stood one on either side of the private entrance to the Jade Room, which did not look like a door at all until you found the handle—not easy for one who had lingered over his liquor. Then there was still one picture, "The Ballet Dancer," which in that long-past age referred to probably inspired more toasts than any other single painting in the world; which turned more men in the direction of art-connoisseuring than any other example of high art known, and whose legs and lingerie caused far more comment and centered more scrutiny than all the cigarette pictures of stage favorites in tights that used to help sell "coffin nails," as they were termed, during the days when "The Ballet Dancer's" reign was being established. On the opposite wall hung a big copy of Paolo Veronese's "Wedding at Cana, in Galilee," for contemplation by those whom liquor put or left in an attitude proper for the contemplation of religious subjects. High above the paneling still hung some of the elks' heads with which the late George C. Boldt, long the old hotel's proprietor, had adorned the place.

But when that laboratory of Bacchic endeavor was in its heyday, pilgrims came from far and wide—from all corners of the globe. They flocked about the rectangular Bar counter and drank deeply of what was good stuff, if not wisdom. As soon as the first bartender appeared in the morning, before even arranging the multitude of glasses of various sizes and shapes on the high stand that took up the central space of the rectangle, he must satisfy the demands of at least half a dozen accumulated patrons, either for breakfast appetizers or for something to take away what was left of the jag of the night before. From five o'clock in the evening until eight, the room was jammed at its tables and at its counter, and late-comers, whose "innards" were sending out an SOS, found themselves impeded in their progress toward satisfaction by S.R.O. conditions.

During those three hours named, the Waldorf-Astoria Bar was Wall Street moved bodily uptown for an adjourned session of the Stock Exchange, with men betting on how stocks would perform the next day. In one discreet corner a ticker kept clicking off news. Here market pools were often formed. Here were to be found men who were willing to bet on anything, and to any amount. Financiers and market operators, with names that gained newspaper front pages every day or so, clustered about the tables, or joined in the maggot-like surge that squirmed for a foothold on the substantial brass tradition that ran along the bottom of the counter. Some who once gained such a post of vantage never left until the Bar closed.

Many forms of beverage dated their origin to the inspiration of some clever Waldorf bartender. Or, perhaps, it was a translation of the passing fancy of a patron who wanted something different to drink, and entirely of his own conception. If the result met his expectations, he might thereafter call only for his own cocktail, or whatever it was, and the bartender, out of compliment, would christen the new drink after its godfather.

A school of drinking, and a distinctive one, the old Waldorf Bar undoubtedly was. And—which may surprise many —it was a real school of art—a school in which more than one connoisseur who has since spent hundreds of thousands in collecting paintings and sculpture, got his first tuition from the pictures on the Bar walls, whose appeal was often emphasized by the cumulative influence of cocktails or highballs.

More than one middle-aged or elderly American who has survived the era that saw bootlegging grow into one of our most important industries, has reason to remember gratefully at least one feature of this particular American School of Drinking, and in which, perhaps, it was preëminent among institutions of similar learning. This was the free lunch table. There are many rich men in this land today, who, were they frank, could date their first acquaintance with Russian caviar to that generous board. There, too, many of them first learned of the superb succulence of Virginia "vintage" ham. As a matter of fact, the exoteric could there give the "once-over" to delicacies they had never before seen—or even imagined. No menu in puzzling French to mystify or confuse. The uninitiate saw what he saw, and what he fancied he could sample at his leisure. And spread out for his delectation—for he was free to choose, and to whatever extent—were light and savory canapés, thirst-provoking anchovies in various-tinted guises, and other delicacies; and there were substantial slices of beef or ham, ordinary as well as Virginia, and a wonderful assortment of cheeses of robust odors; not forgetting the crisp radishes and sprightly, delicate spring onions, and olives stuffed and unstuffed.

The temporary addicts of the lunch table were never disturbed, or rarely. Their meal ticket depended merely upon good conduct—supported, of course, by a good front. The occasional investment of a quarter in a bottle of beer

—not necessarily spent before an attack upon the lunch table—served to keep them in good standing. By such an outlay as little as three times a week, a man could eat daily from that hospitable offering a luncheon that, served in one of the hotel's restaurants, would have set him back a good two dollars—and get away with it. And many so did. The table in the Waldorf-Astoria Bar cost the hotel more than seventy-five hundred dollars a year. It proved excellent advertisement, for no inconsiderable slice of the hotel's profits came from the sale of wines and liquors.

Service was rendered with a distinction many establishments of a similar nature lacked. For example, in its early days, a small, snowy napkin went with each drink, enabling a patron to remove certain traces from his mustache or his whiskers—heavy mustaches and whiskers were abundant—without toting home odors in his hip pocket, or wherever he carried his handkerchief. And while questions were not usually asked, men who bought drinks were supposed to be able to freight them away intact, and not to spill them, or to show other effects than a certain mellowness and good fellowship—though perhaps fluency in argument or reminiscence might be forgiven one who was standing treat. In brief, a gentleman was supposed to be larger than what he drank. The theory of the proprietor of the establishment was that all his patrons were gentlemen. And the theory was good, even if it didn't always work out in practice.

The actual bar itself, a large, rectangular counter at the northeast corner of the room, as noted, had a brass rail running all around its foot. In its center was a long refrigerator topped by a snowy cloth and an orderly arrangement of drinking glasses. At one end of this cover stood a good-sized bronze bear, looking as if it meant business; at the other end, a rampant bull. Midway between them was placed a tiny lamb, flanked on either side by a tall vase of flowers. The whole decoration was a more or less delicate compliment to the heaviest patronage of the room at cocktail-time, wags claiming that the flowers were all the lamb—the innocent public—got after Wall Street's bulls and bears had finished with him.

To name the important figures that were to be seen at various times in that Barroom during its first fifteen or twenty years would be like setting down most of the names from various editions of Who's Who in America—excepting, of course, always preachers—and including a good-sized list taken from the British Who's Who and the Almanach de Gotha. As a gathering place for celebrities, the room was one of the real sights of New York. But in recollection, one cannot stop to assign faces to a particular period. There is too nearly a sea of them.

While Colonel William F. Cody—"Buffalo Bill"—clung to the old Hoffman House as long as his friend, Ed. Stokes, was its proprietor, he used to drop into the Waldorf Bar, and there one might discover him at a table surrounded by a lot of admirers.

Cody, with his wide-brimmed hat, long mustache and goatee, and in the old days wearing a Prince Albert coat, presented a handsome figure and one which eyes seldom failed to follow.

Men liked to invite Colonel Cody to "have one" with them, and it is not on record that he ever refused. In accepting such an invitation, he followed an invariable formula.

"Sir," he would respond heartily, "you speak the language of my tribe."

John W. Gates, of "Betcha-a-million" fame, and his bosom friend, Colonel "Ike" Ellwood, appeared in the Bar, occasionally, though Gates' favorite hangout was the Men's Café, across the hall. With them when he came to New York almost invariably trailed Colonel John Lambert, sometime warden of Joliet, Ill., penitentiary, but president of the American Steel & Wire Company at the time of the formation of the Steel Trust. In the Gates aura, too, one would discover John A. Drake and the latter's brother-in-law, Theodore P. Shonts—that was before he was made chairman of the Panama Canal Commission— and Loyall L. Smith, a millionaire who had once been a Chicago newsboy. And while its owner was a strict tee-totaler, the round face of Diamond Jim Brady, brass fittings salesman, gormand and dinner-party impresario, could be seen circulating among the crowd, as he button-holed this or that "Big Feller," the orb illuminated by forty to a hundred carats of diamonds or emeralds, or sapphires, or whatnot, that glowed or gleamed from an expansive shirt-front or a particularly noisy necktie.

What now seems an almost incredible proportion of the brokers and operators in the Wall Street of twenty-five to thirty years ago—at least such as were family men—had homes in the immediate vicinity of the Waldorf, Westchester and Long Island and uptown apartments not yet having come into widespread vogue as dwelling places for Wall Street. "Cocktail-hour" drew a real majority of them to the Waldorf Bar. Whether they drank or not, there they knew they would find men they wished to see.

Many of these cocktail-hour patrons were hosts at tables. As a rule, they actually drank cocktails at that time, Martinis being most popular and Manhattans running second. That was before the "Clover Club" had won in New York temples of thirst a wide but short-lived popularity. Very few fancy drinks were served at cocktail-time. There were many customers, who would stand up to the bar with a group of friends, and before they moved away would gulp down five or six Manhattans or Martinis in succession. A big banquet in the hotel would fill the Barroom at midnight, for whatever they had had upstairs of cocktails, champagne, and liqueurs, many men must have, in those days, a nightcap. Often, it took several to get them properly "head-dressed" for bed.

Not infrequently, revolution-experts were of the company present—men who were the heads or members of organizations that stood ready, at the drop of a hat, or upon receipt of a code cable, to start up trouble in any Latin-American country, provided the price was forthcoming. Gun-running was at one time a remunerative, if sometime hazardous vocation—some spelled it "avocation"—in the Caribbean and along the West coast from Nicaragua down. One dealer in ammunition and guns owned, or leased, an island up the Hudson, which was reported to be well stocked with the latest war material of the day. This could be promptly dumped into the hold of a chartered "tramp" and headed wherever trouble was brewing.

Every gold rush was followed sooner or later by an influx of rough-looking men wearing wide-brimmed hats— and more than once, cowhide boots—and the air would resound with tales of "big strikes" and of "prospects" that promised big, and whose performances later made a big hole in many a speculative bank account. Cripple Creek, for example; Alaska, Tonopah—all paid tribute to Boldt's

Bar. And those miners wanted the most expensive drinks. Champagne was their first thought.

More than once a flood of reminiscence, developed through continuous imbibition, and the cropping up of some subject that had been, or was possibly still disputable among the men from the Still-Open Spaces, threatened trouble. At least once a swift train of events beginning with a slighting reference to the virtue, valor and discretion of "Bat" Masterson succeeded in starting a panic in the Bar, because of the sudden materialization of the subject of the reference, backed by his reputation for saying the last word, and with a "gun."

"Bat" Masterson, a United States Marshal, long famous in the Northwest, and a friend of Theodore Roosevelt, was in New York at the time, but not in the hotel, when the thing started that, after he did come in, was effective in holding up trade and leaving the bartenders on duty keeping company only with the bull and the bear and the lamb on top the refrigerator table.

At a table in the middle of the room sat six big men, some of them in wide-brimmed hats. Most of them were mining men, and they were from Butte, Montana. Of the group was Colonel "Dick" Plunkett, said to be a United States Marshal.

They were talking about gold strikes, mining conditions and individual exploits, law and order, jumping claims, and other things mining men usually discussed at such gatherings. Not a little egocentric hero-worship was voiced, but the talk was mostly of what other fellows had done; of "bad men" and shootings. And Masterson's name was mentioned as having saved the expense of a lot of hangings by using his six-shooter.

Plunkett dissented. He was emphatic about it.

"I tell you what," he said, "that fellow, Bat Masterson, has killed more innocent men in his day than anybody else in the United States!"

Whether the statement was immediately challenged or not, is not recorded. Masterson had good friends in that group. A little later, one of them made an excuse and left the room. He knew where Bat was, and he got into a hansom and ordered the driver to go there, lickety-split. And he gave a news-hot version of what Plunkett had said.

Hardly half an hour after the statement had been made, Masterson in person dramatically appeared at the main door of the Barroom. One of the men at the table caught sight of him and jumped up. The others, following his gaze, turned. Two or three right hands went to hips.

Bat, after halting long enough to achieve sensational effect, strode straight across to the group. He stopped at the side of his detractor's chair.

"Plunkett," he said, "I hear you have been talking bad about me." With the words, he suddenly dug his hand between Colonel Dick's neck and collar, shut his fist, and made as if to pull the other out of his chair.

Plunkett was conciliatory. "Sit down, Bat," he said; "sit down and have a quiet drink, and talk things over."

Then a man on his other side jumped up. "Take your hands off my friend, Dick Plunkett!" he shouted at Masterson, at the same time trying to jerk something from his hip pocket.

Meantime, the effect upon the crowd had been panicky. Immediately the identity of Masterson had begun to be whispered about. "That's Bat Masterson," men told one another. "He'll shoot on sight," some added. So before

Masterson had grabbed Plunkett's collar, a movement had started toward the exit—toward all exits, in fact. Men began pouring not only into the extension of Peacock Alley, but into the Grill Room, and the emergency lavatory at the southeast corner of the Bar, past which safety could be gained, was choked by men who merely wanted to find a quick way out, but missed the door.

Opportunities offered by the assemblage of so many men who were making easy money in mining, or in "The Street," were too pregnant to be resisted by certain purveyors of luxuries. At least one noted dealer in uncut precious stones always drifted in to scan those whose actions or talk indicated they had been lucky in the market, and he usually did a thriving business because, in those times, men who had made money on "flyers" were apt to have their lighter moments. That crafty psychologist derived considerable profit from persuading such that one way to celebrate their good fortune was to select a costly trinket for the lady in the uptown flat. And invariably in the gathering were to be discovered a full half-dozen gentlemen whose specialty in trade was either high-priced art or antiques. To their activities amid those inspirational scenes one who used to know most of the local art merchants and many of the imported ones has often dated the rise of the passion for art-collecting which became so widespread and violent during the early years of the century. More than once, however, the yearning for the acquisition of "high art" instilled—or distilled—in that impregnated, if not perfumed, atmosphere, was subjected to check and revision by experience and acquired knowledge of the subject; and more than one *nouveau* who used to brag about the "old masters" he had picked up, found excuse later on to subject his art gallery to a process of weeding.

To dismiss a recollection of a place where much rude, ungainly and uproarious story-telling was done, but where, too, so much real humor came out under the stimulative effect of generously drunk spirit, without calling to mind one of its most decorative as well as most intelligent wits, would almost mean leaving the best egg out of this rum omelet. Up rises from a table at the farther end of the room a tall, slender man whose gray mustache bears evidence that the lingering traces of good liquor may be held too precious for desecration by a pocket handkerchief.

"Private John Allen to the bar!"

And "Private" John Allen never said nay to such an invitation.

The way he used to tell it, Congressman Allen—of Tupelo, Mississippi, suh!—had dubbed himself with the title by which he was invariably known. After the Civil War he found the South overrun with generals and colonels and majors, so that at encampments of Confederate veterans, when it seemed that everybody he met had commanded an army, a brigade, a regiment, or at least a battalion, while he himself had never risen above the ranks, he concluded he must be the only private of the Confederate Army who had survived the conflict. So he chose for himself the title of "Private," and thereafter gave it distinction.

Private Allen showed up at least once a year at the Waldorf, and his visits seldom continued less than three weeks. One afternoon, his friend, Colonel E. T. Brown of Atlanta, arrived at the hotel and, suspecting the whereabouts of his intimate, sought the door of the Bar. And, sure enough, at his favorite table, the center of a group of attentive listeners, sat Private John Allen. On the table was a bottle of Old Green River whiskey. At Allen's right was a stout man, red-faced and with a tremendous mustache of a hue that matched. The other waved his hand and shouted, "Come right over, Colonel Brown!" As the newcomer approached, Private John arose.

"Gentlemen," he said, "this is Colonel Brown, of Atlanta, Georgia. Colonel Brown, suh, I wish you to meet Majah Soandso. Majah Soandso is the representative, suh, of that wonderful, that potent, that seductive beverage—O-l-d Gre-e-n Rivah."

Colonel Brown sat and the bottle was passed around. Another was ordered and then another. Finally, Private John suggested: "Let's all go down to the Hoffman House."

A few minutes later, the party lined up at the long bar counter of that establishment.

"Gentlemen, will you indicate your preference?" Private John's voice invited. Each named his choice in turn. Finally the white-coated bartender reached the end of the line.

"And yours, sir?" he said to Private John.

"You may give me, suh," came the answer in a full, round voice that reverberated through the room, "some of that great liquah that is considered a boon in every well-regulated household—O-l-d Gr-e-en Rivah!"

The bartender inclined his head to one side. "I beg your pardon, sir," he said. "I didn't quite catch that."

"I said, suh," Private John returned, "some of that beneficent, luscious, pervasive and persuasive liquah whose eloquence has chahmed a continent—O-l-l-d Gr-r-e-e-en Rivah!"

"I am very sorry, sir," the polite barman now returned, shaking his head. "We haven't such whiskey and I have never heard of it. But we have Old Crow, Y.P.M.—"

"What, suh?" bellowed Private Allen. "Do you mean to tell me, suh, that you haven't any of that famous, soul-inspirin' liquah; the joy of every American father, the pride of every American mother, and for which American children cry instead of for Pitchah's Castoria—O-l-l-l-d G-r-r-r-e-e-n Rivah?"

"I am sorry, sir," said the barman, "but we haven't it."

"Well, by Gawd," exclaimed Private Allen, his voice this time at its highest and most reverberant pitch, "you haven't got Old Green Rivah! Well, suh, I just refuse to drink in such a low-down place. Come on, fellahs!" And he led the way out of the barroom.

The next afternoon, Colonel Brown saw Private Allen and the red-mustached major in close communion just outside the Barroom entrance. The major slipped away. Private John said to Colonel Brown, with a chuckle, "Do you know, the Majah tells me he slipped into the Hoffman House Bar, this mornin', and sold 'em seventy-five cases of Old Green Rivah. Colonel," he continued, with a wink, "how'd you like, suh, for me to send you down to Atlanta a case of Old Green Rivah with my compliments?"

SOME THINGS MOST PEOPLE DON'T
KNOW ABOUT LIQUORS

FOR the benefit of antiquarians and serious students of American *mores*—as well as for the information of those who like to know what's in a name or two, when applied to liquor—the author has deemed it expedient to append a brief Glossary, which may serve to uncork certain useful and perhaps entertaining particulars concerning spirits and other things mentioned in the Formulary portion of this book.

To begin with, take "Berries." As used in the text, "Berries," it should be emphasized, does not mean dollars—simply small fruit usually growing on vines or diminutive plants. "Mug," as employed, does not signify a face, or "to photograph," as commonly applied these days; but a container made of glass, crockery, or stone, with a handle, and used for dispensing ale, cider, or, infrequently, beer. A "lemon" is a small yellow fruit; and "lemon peel," of course, is the rind.

The word "Egg," as frequently used, should be taken in a literal and primitive sense. In the days when recipes were written down in the Old Bar Book, the term "Pittsburgh Steel Millionaire" had not yet been synonymously superseded in Manhattanese by "Big Butter and Egg Man," and at the Old Waldorf Bar "Good Egg" was synchronous and synonymous with "Fresh Egg." Whatever metaphorical or sinister sense either has come later to assume, each then meant simply a natural output of a female of the chicken species, and in fair condition. A "Nutmeg" was, and still is, the aromatic kernel of the fruit of a tree of the *Myristica* family.

"Cock's Comb" as used, meant literally what it says, however incredible to those who think only of a cow or a goat when they return to the barnyard for something to drink. As an elective concomitant, if not an ingredient, of the Chanticleer cocktail, a Cock's Comb was a ruddy, serrated, distinctive capital decoration peculiar to the masculine chicken. It was pickled or bottled as a sweetmeat in France, often with other elemental components of departed roosters, particularly what are known to high-class grocers and certain gourmets as *"Financières."* The Cock's Comb and the *Financière* are still reputed among the ultra-sophisticated to possess virtues akin to those of certain simian appropriations recommended by a distinguished Slavic surgeon. Indeed, the manager of one well-known mart for rare comestibles and delicacies stoutly maintained to the writer that the combination is in great and growing demand.

"Ginger ale" is now perhaps even better known than in pre-prohibition days, so it should be unnecessary to define it, except so far as to say that "imported" ginger ale used to mean that the product had been manufactured in some other country than the United States. An "orange," of course, signified about what it does today, though "orange peel" used to mean a good deal more, as in the compendium there will be found numerous concoctions in which it was used for flavoring purposes. "Mint," a pungent herb commonly found in kitchen gardens, has long filled a noble office in certain parts of this country—particularly below Mason and Dixon's line, and most notably, perhaps, in Kentucky, though in other states great pride is exhibited by many citizens in the virtues of a compound whose recipe, they claim, has been handed down in some particular family for generations past. In recent years and in New York, it seems to have become more closely identified with the chewing gum industry than anything else. It might be emphasized that when the Old Waldorf recipes were compiled, the word "raspberry" had not become synonymous with "horse's laugh" or any other anatomical performance and the expression "give him the raspberry" had not come into common use. Nor had "strawberries" entered the realm of slang. Berries were berries and fruits were fruits. It was a simpler age.

A few processes employed by bar-mixers of the old American School, and named here and there, seem to call for some clarification.

For example, to "muddle" meant to mash and stir up one or more ingredients, and had no objective reference to the person who was getting the drink; to "cup" meant either to shape or use as a cup, or to place in the bottom of a cup or glass; to "frappé" meant to cool with ice. More frequently than not, a bartender averse to the vigorous and more than local exercise demanded by plying a cocktail-shaker achieved a similar effect by the finger-and-wrist method of gently stirring a few lumps of ice with a spoon, but, as already intimated, "stirring" was often prescribed in the formula.

With this brief introduction, one passes on to the Glossary proper. The definitions are confined to terms used in the compendium. The term "voltage," given where it is known, signifies "horse-power," "kick," or "alcoholic content," and is used as being more in accord with this age of electricity.

DEFINITIONS

ABSINTHE—Usually a green, bitter, aromatic liquor, impregnated with wormwood, though there was also a white variety manufactured in France. *Deriv.*, Latin, *absinthium*, "wormwood." Long a resort for parodists in such lines as "Absinthe makes the heart grow fonder." Taken "neat" and often, was guaranteed to produce visions of snakes, etc. Voltage, 58.93.

ANISETTE—A liquor made in France by distillation from anise seed. Voltage, 42.

APPLEJACK—Often used synonymously with apple brandy or apple whiskey and supposed to be a distillation. New Jersey continued producing the one—or the three—right through prohibition.

AROMATIC SPIRITS OF AMMONIA.—A fragrant distillation from a colorless, pungent, suffocating gas (NH_3) obtained from nitrogenous organic bodies, such as coal, bones, blood, etc.

BENEDICTINE—A cordial or liqueur, distilled for centuries at Fécamp, in France, by the Benedictine monks. Its composition was kept secret and some persons believed its distillation was accompanied by religious rites. However, after the French Revolution, discovery was made that it could be produced by the laity and by strictly secular methods. Its components have been kept a trade secret, but it was believed to contain the volatile constituents of cardamom seeds, arnica flowers, angelica

root, lemon peel, thyme, nutmegs, cassia, hyssop, peppermint, and cloves. Imitation of Benedictine is not so
much confined to prohibition history as patrons of bootleggers may have become convinced. As a matter of fact,
such has been going on in France and elsewhere for generations, the average customer who did not know being
satisfied if the bottle was queer and squat and bore the
initials "D.O.M." Voltage, 52.

BITTERS—Beverages containing alcohol, together with a
component for cathartic effect. Best known varieties:
Angostura, made from the bark of a South American
tree; Calisaya, synonymous with cinchona or quinine,
also of South American origin; Orange; Boonekamp,
made in Germany; Boker's, Amer Picon (which a ste-
nographer rendered for me "American Pecan," but which
is really a French proprietary proposition); Hostetter's,
West Indies, Pepsin, Peychaud (formerly made in New
Orleans); Fernet Branca, etc. So named from the usual
bitter taste.

BRANDY—(Sometimes called "cognac," from a town in
France noted for its manufacture.) Alcoholic liquor distilled from wine. *Deriv.*, Dutch, *brandewijn*, meaning
"burnt wine." Was also made from the juice of apri-
cots, peaches, apples or other fruit by distillation, and
called liqueur. Cognac was often called for by the
name of its maker, though in other days it was often
referred to by the symbol printed on its label, "★ ★ ★"
or "★ ★ ★ ★ ★," as indulgers frequently proved unable
to read when ready for an encore. Voltage, 53.4.

CHARTREUSE—A distillation with brandy of certain
rare herbs, used as a cordial or liqueur. The name was
derived from the fact that Chartreuse, like Benedictine,

owed its invention to early French monks, who knew about what they wanted and got it. These monks were of the Carthusian Order, and the liqueur was made only at their monastery in the Grande Chartreuse, in the French Alps. The formula for its preparation was said to be known only to the Father Superior of the Order. When the monks were expelled from France, in 1903, they spirited the secret of its preparation to Tarragona, in Spain, whence comes an herb much esteemed by gourmets in the treatment of vinegar. Rival manufactories were then set up in France, but their product was never so good as the original brand. Some thirty years or so before their expulsion, the Carthusian monks had suffered a big loss in the destruction of their brandy warehouses, wherein was stored what was said to be the largest stock of old Napoleon brandy in existence. Even before prohibition came, as much as twenty dollars a bottle was paid in New York for Chartreuse dated 1869 or before. While the monks have kept their formula a secret, analysts have named among the ingredients of Chartreuse: balm leaves, orange peel, dried hyssop tops, peppermint, wormwood, angelica seed and root, cinnamon, mace, cloves, Tonka beans, *calamus aromaticus* and cardamom. Some of the flavor, if not virtues of the product, however, was ascribed to certain herbs which were said to grow only in the neighborhood of the Grande Chartreuse. There were three varieties of Chartreuse—yellow, green, and white. Voltage, 43.

COINTREAU—A liqueur made in France, but not well known in the United States before prohibition.

CRÈME DE CACAO—An extract of cocoa, made in France. Used as a cordial or liqueur.

CRÈME DE CASSIS—A liqueur made in France of black currants, whose voltage still causes headaches to some who recall its potency.

CRÈME DE MENTHE—A distillation of mint, or of brandy flavored with mint. Usually green in color, though there is also a white variety. By those who could not pronounce its name correctly, it was often called "green mint," or "white mint," *menthe* being the French word for "mint." It is usually made in France. Voltage, 48.

CRÈME YVETTE—An extract of violets, used for flavoring purposes; also drunk as a cordial or liqueur. Its perfume often gave it preference over the common or garden refuge of the drinking dissembler—a clove or peppermint lozenge—before the commercial discovery of halitosis. Made in New York.

CURAÇAO—Often mispronounced "Curacoa," especially by Englishmen. A liquor made by distilling spirits with orange peel and certain spices. Manufactured originally in Holland. Name derived from that of a Dutch island off the north coast of South America. Voltage, 55.

DUBONNET—A proprietary French bitters or tonic, one of whose ingredients is said to be quinine.

GIN—Originally a drink distilled from malt or other grain and afterwards rectified with and flavored with juniper berries. Manufactured in Holland, under the name of Hollands, Schiedam, and Schnapps. For the effect of Schnapps, see Washington Irving's tale of that sterling New Yorker of pre-war times, *Rip Van Winkle.* Also manufactured in England under various names, notably: Gordon, Booth's, Holloway's, Old Tom, Nicholson, Plymouth, House of Lords, etc. Among the lower classes of London, "gin" is alcohol, flavored with oil of turpentine and common salt. The term is often used generically for "bad liquor." In some parts of the Cotton Belt, "gin" signifies a beverage whose effects are momentarily synonymous with those produced by the saws of a cotton gin—from which it is *not* derived. The actual derivation is from the Dutch *jenever*, itself coming from the old French word *jenevre*, meaning juniper. Gin was sometimes called "Geneva," or "Geneva Water," and ascribed to Swiss invention. Voltage, 54.3.

SLOE GIN—Not to be confused with the real gin, and it should be noted that as compared with real gin, its effects are described by its first name, differently spelled. Sloe Gin is a sort of cordial made by distillation from the small, plum-like astringent fruit of the Blackthorn, or a distillation flavored with the same.

GRAND MARNIER—A cordial, or liqueur, made in France from oranges.

GRENADINE—A red syrup or cordial, said to be made from pomegranates; manufactured in France.

KIRSCH or KIRSCHWASSER—A liquor distilled from European wild cherries, and made in Germany and other central European countries.

KÜMMEL or KIMMEL—A liquor made generally from highly rectified alcohol, flavored with cumin (a plant of the parsley family) and caraway seeds. Before the War it was manufactured chiefly at Riga, then in Russia. Voltage, 33.9.

MARASCHINO (pronounced "maraskeeno")—A cordial distilled from fermented cherries and flavored with bruised pits. *Deriv.*, Italian, *marasquino*.

OJEN—A cordial formerly made in New Orleans, La.,

and flavored with absinthe.

ORGEAT—A syrup made in France from sugar, orange flower water and almonds. *Deriv.*, French, from Latin, *hordeum*, barley.

PARFAIT D'AMOUR—A red cordial whose composition was a proprietary secret, but whose name often assured those who had a slight acquaintance with French that it was a sort of love potion.

RUM—Generally, the name of any alcoholic liquor. Used as an adjective, colloquial English for "queer" or "peculiar." Specifically, an alcoholic liquor distilled from fermented molasses, or cane juice. Varieties usually named from country of origin—Jamaica, Swedish, St. Croix (West Indies), Cuban—better known as Bacardi or Santiago—and Japanese (usually called Sake and distilled from fermented rice). *Deriv.*, abbreviation of "rumbullion" or "rumbooze." The latter term is composed of the gypsy word *rom* or *rum*, meaning "good," and "booze," a corruption of the Dutch *bouse*, meaning to "guzzle," but now used as a good English word with a sinister meaning. The manufacture of rum was at one time an important New England industry, antedating that of cotton cloth. Voltage, 53.7. See "Jamaican Jollifiers."

SHERRY—Originally meant the white wine of Jerez, Spain, from whose name it was derived. Jerez was pronounced "Hareth," or "Herreth." The English corruption may have been due to excessive sibilance manifested by the original Britisher who drank a bottle and demanded more. Voltage, 19.

SODA, SIPHON, PLAIN SODA, CARBONIC, SELTZER, VICHY—Water charged with gas and discharged into a glass by pressing a lever controlling the metal vent of a siphon. CLUB SODA, aerated water in a small bottle. LEMON SODA, the same with a flavor of synthetic lemon. DELATOUR SODA, a brand of a particular manufacturer. The word VICHY was a misnomer, appropriated from that of the famous water bottled at Vichy, France, by the French Government.

SWEDISH PUNSCH—A beverage manufactured in Sweden, and having somewhat of the taste and properties of Rum. Voltage, 26.3.

VERMOUTH—A liquor made from white wine, flavored with aromatic herbs. Formerly, of the two varieties, the Italian, or sweet, was made in Italy, and the French, or *sec* (dry), was manufactured in France. A *sec* Vermouth is also made in Italy. *Deriv.*, German, *wermuth*, meaning "wormwood." In the country of its origin, Vermouth is often drunk "neat," that is to say, unmixed with water or more potent liquids. Voltage, about 17.

VIN MARIANI—A wine made in France from cocoa, and formerly very much advertised as a tonic.

WHISKEY—Again less comprehensive in definition than of late years, whiskey is an alcoholic liquor obtained by the distillation of a fermented starchy compound, usually a grain. *Deriv.*, Gaelic, *uisgebeatha*, "water of life." It used to be called also *eau de vie* or *aqua vitae*, meaning the same as the Gaelic term. The Swedes appropriated the name for "Aquavit," now one of their national drinks. Varieties: rye whiskey, made from that product; corn whiskey, called "Bourbon" if manufactured in Kentucky, and blended with rye, but turned out as "White Mule," "Moonshine" and under other names in illicit

distilleries throughout the South; "Scotch," named for
the country of its origin and popularly supposed to be
made of oatmeal, the national dish, turned into spirits
by the aid of peat fires, but more probably of barley or
other grain, and "Irish," made in Ireland.

WINE—The juice of grapes, fermented by nature, in
course of time. Varieties named in the compendium in-
clude Claret, the ordinary red wine of certain districts in
France (voltage, 13.3); Burgundy, the heavy red wine
of Bourgogne, France (voltage, 13.6); Madeira, the
wine of the Portuguese Island of that name; Port, a
wine whose name came from the Portuguese city of
Oporto, whence it was exported; Rhine, meaning a wine
made of grapes grown in the Rhine valley; Beaune,
wines both red and white, made in the vicinity of
Beaune, France, and about the same voltage as Burgundy; Bordeaux, made of grapes grown in the territory contiguous to the city of Bordeaux, France (voltage,
11.5); Champagne, an effervescent wine made before
the war in the Marne region of France, particularly at
Rheims (voltage, 12.2).

BAR GLASSES—Among the glasses mentioned as proper
for the service of the fancy potations, the name "star"
appears frequently. According to surviving authorities
on bar-containers of the period, a "star" was synonymous
with a SOUR glass.

The SOUR glass, so called because it was used for
"sours" of various kinds, held from five and a half to
six ounces. The LEMONADE was originally a thick goblet,
but in time it became a thin, straight-sided glass, holding
from six to eight ounces. The latter was originally the
same as a FIZZ or a HIGH-BALL glass. The COLLINS

started out by being an eight-ounce glass, but a demand for a longer drink led to the adoption of a twelve- or even a sixteen-ounce glass—one that, besides the gin and the ice, would hold a "split" of soda. The CHAMPAGNE was usually a wide-bowled, thin-stemmed goblet; often, however, a thin four-ounce tumbler, was also used, the same being also called an APOLLINARIS glass. A SHERRY glass was a small glass with a sharp, conical bowl, holding from three-quarters of an ounce to about an ounce and a third. A PONY was identical with a small liqueur glass, and held a scant ounce. A POUSSE CAFÉ glass was an elongated pony, holding about an ounce and a half. A WHISKEY was a thin, low, straight-sided vessel holding about four ounces. The CLARET, a thin goblet, held from three and a half to four ounces.

The JIGGER was a conical metal container, holding about two ounces. In many establishments its use was abandoned in favor of the barman's eye. He was supposed to be able to gauge a jiggerful when pouring from a bottle in composing mixed drinks. In first class establishments, the customer was usually permitted to measure his own whiskey when he took it "heat," or in a high-ball.